CHRISTIANITY ACCORDING TO PAUL

STUDIES IN BIBLICAL THEOLOGY · 49

CHRISTIANITY ACCORDING TO PAUL

MICHEL BOUTTIER

WIPF & STOCK · Eugene Oregon

Wipf and Stock Publishers
199 W 8th Ave, Suite 3
Eugene, OR 97401

Christianity According to Paul
By Bouttier, Michel
Copyright©1966 SCM Press
ISBN 13: 978-1-60899-027-6
Publication date 9/22/2009
Previously published by SCM Press, 1966

Copyright © SCM Press 1965
First English edition 1965 by SCM Press
This Edition published by arrangement with SCM-Canterbury Press

CONTENTS

Foreword by Professor C. F. D. Moule   7
Preface   9
Abbreviations   13

I   THE CHRISTIAN CONDITION   15
The orientation of Paul's existence. Phil. 3.4–21.
Being conformed to the death and resurrection of Jesus Christ. A paradoxical condition. Growth and eschatology. Dependence.

II   COMMUNION WITH CHRIST   32
1. Union with Christ. The historical existence of Jesus as the source of our life.
2. Waiting for Christ. Postponement. The meeting with the Lord.
3. Christ's presence. Life hidden with Christ in God. Life manifested in us by the Spirit. Christ's presence a sign of the realization of God's plan. A gift offered for others. Education in sonship.
4. The imitation of Christ. An 'apostolic succession'.

III   COMMUNION IN CHRIST   59
Living together in Jesus Christ.
1. In you as in Christ. Sharing in common. Baptism (I Cor. 12.13; Gal. 3.26–29; Col. 3.9–11). Welcome. The Lord's Supper.
2. Death and life, suffering and comfort. Strength and weakness. Their correlation. Col. 1.24.
3. *Agapē*

IV   LIFE IN CHRIST AND A NEW CREATION   92
1. The Body of Christ and a new creation. The new creature. II Cor. 5.17. The reality, the Body of Christ. Inheritance. First fruits. The end of the Church. The testimony of Colossians and Ephesians.
2. Newness of life. The Body of Christ and ethics. Holiness. Kingship. Freedom.
3. Recapitulation.

Contents

CONCLUSION	118
Bibliography	120
Index of Authors	123
Index of Biblical References	125

FOREWORD

It gives me pleasure to be allowed to write a foreword to this book. When M. Bouttier's earlier book *En Christ*, published in 1962, arrived on my desk for review, I knew nothing about the author; but it quickly became evident that, whoever he was, he brought a distinguished mind to bear on one of the most delicate and most discussed of all Pauline phrases, and had succeeded in throwing fresh light on its variegated meanings and nuances. The review I ultimately wrote brought us into friendly correspondence with one another, and there followed the gift of the French original of the present book which seeks to apply some of the results of the previous more academic and more closely linguistic study to an elucidation of St Paul's religion.

Perhaps the sort of New Testament scholar most needed today is the one who can apply his learning objectively to the tangled phenomena of first-century Greek and, at the same time, can piece the results together with the insights of an experienced pastor and the liveliness which is lent by wide-ranging interests. In his first letter to me M. Bouttier made some apology for having had to do the work on *En Christ* in the midst of distracting pastoral duties. Similarly in his introduction to the present book he alludes to a distracting wartime situation. But I suspect that the scholar with such a background finds, now that a measure of academic scope has come his way, that, in fact, his work gains enormously in depth and sensitiveness as a result of these past experiences, and that what may, at the time, have seemed frustrating turns out to be no small gain. At any rate, here is a book by an academic who is not only an academic.

M. Bouttier will not necessarily carry his readers all the way in all his exegesis; but no thoughtful reader can fail to be stimulated. Consider, as one random sample, the years of cogitation that are concerned—for writer and reader alike—in the footnote on pp. 47f. This author's expositions seem always to be based on very careful linguistic study and profound thought, and they are alive with a sense of their importance for real life: and that is what

Foreword

makes a book like this a notable contribution to the understanding both of St Paul's inner life and of how to live *in Christo* now.

C. F. D. MOULE

Cambridge
5 April 1965

PREFACE

THE origin of this work, if a date has to be fixed, goes back a long time. One evening, in a university service, during my student days amid the general confusion of the war, I heard a fellow student read these striking words, which brought an unhoped-for response: 'For me to live is Christ'. The apostle Paul brought about a close-forged union between that name, which I already loved but was perhaps keeping back in the recesses of my heart, and an existence that was opening before me but now seemed to have no meaning for my contemporaries.

Why did that call awaken so few echoes? On the one hand, believers hardly seemed anxious to make their way into a life lived in Christ, but were satisfied to stay on the threshold, the point of the break-through, the moment of conversion at which the preachers left them, as if the revelation stopped short at that point. The rest, for their part, remained untouched by the apostle's response. Pursuing moving but inconclusive discussions of which we have fragments in Simone de Beauvoir's *Mandarins*, they rejected a light that would have dispelled their contradictions—and were they not right? Was I the victim of a myth, of an experience which, however authentic, had grown stale down the centuries? Thus I had to look through the eyes of those who, like me, had entrusted their lives to the Lord, and also of those who were made to realize by the moving words of a Camus that they themselves were not really committed to their own adventure.

It was a piece of university work that led me towards the problems of Pauline mysticism, and this brought me to study the expression *in Christo*—a study that was many times left and taken up again, and was completed, in its first form, in the exegetical sketch recently published.[1] I hope now to make use of some of its results; I have sought, by strict attention to grammar and philology, to grasp more closely the reality that is at once hidden and revealed at the heart of Paul's writings. Life in Christ must

[1] *En Christ*, étude d'exégèse et de théologie pauliniennes, Presses Universitaires, Paris, 1962.

Preface

not be detached from exegesis and theology; least of all must we be left to the chances of our own experiences or to the mercy of personal or ecclesiastical situations. The more life touches the mysteries of divine communion, and the more it reaches the depths of God, the more necessary is it to be strictly faithful to his word. Let us admit that the believer is too often abandoned on the threshold of the new life with nothing more than a few vague or sentimental hints, as if its mystical nature were beyond words; or perhaps he has certain principles laid down for him, so that he once more puts himself under the yoke of a law. Paul shows us admirably that we must by all means avoid both illuminism and legalism. The law of the old covenant has been succeeded by the reign of the Spirit, but the action of that Spirit is never separated from the person of Christ, who has himself been fully revealed to us. We are 'under the law of Christ' (I Cor. 9.21): he remains, through the Spirit, the final authority for our behaviour; and although this authority remains sovereign, it is living, and is neither foreign nor external. That is the nature of life in Christ—not a rule of thumb, not an intangible and fugitive illumination, but a self-giving reality to be known, and to which one can only bear witness; the Pauline letters take on the aspect of another Genesis in which this second creation was revealed emerging from the chaos of the world.

It will be noticed, however, that we have avoided using the phrase 'life in Christ' as a title, though not its use in the text; the expression, although it is suitable to our purpose, is not met with in this particular form in the apostle's writings; he avoids all such abstract phrases; he is careful not to allow that life to appear as a reality in itself to be added to that of salvation, except so as to raise it to a higher level. Forgiveness, justification, reconciliation, life, are found in the letters like facets of one single gospel, and are not to be dissociated from one another. And if there is one conclusion that we seem to reach, it is that life in Christ is bound up with the existence of Jesus of Nazareth as with the glorious appearance of the Son of man. By this the personal relation with him, far from being broken, is confirmed. We shall pursue this first of all, but it will be found, in its turn, inseparable from the human relations that embody it, as are our daily existence and eternal life.

Preface

But how are we to set out on paper that three-dimensional space, where the present is rooted in the past and goes out into the future? If before we can dissect a body we have to take from it the breath that animates it, how can our analysis fail to break up and destroy the complex and moving reality of life in Christ as revealed to us by the apostle and unveiled through him? The theologian would willingly efface himself behind the poet who alone is able to suggest faithfully what is not to be demonstrated, and to evoke what is not to be explained. We shall approach the subject from one direction, then from another, disclaiming at the outset any idea of including everything, and outlining some of the themes which, like open routes, will allow the reader to get some inkling of the promises of this life, and to go forward towards the one who is its secret.

Lyons   MICHEL BOUTTIER
15 October 1961

NOTE: For convenience, we have kept the Latin transcription *in Christo* of Paul's wording. We beg the reader to excuse the inevitable cross-referencing from the present work to our former one.

We have tried to use language that everyone can understand, and to have as little recourse as possible to Greek and to references. The reader may be surprised by some exegetical excursuses; we have felt obliged to undertake these when the way had not been prepared by previous study and where we therefore had to justify our assertions.

ABBREVIATIONS

Blass   Blass and Debrunner, *Grammatik des neutestamentlichen Griechisch*, 8th ed., Göttingen, 1949
CNT   Commentaire du Nouveau Testament, Neuchâtel:
       VI. F. J. Leenhardt, *L'épître de saint Paul aux Romains*, 1957
       VII. J. Héring, *La première épître de saint Paul aux Corinthiens*, 1949
       VIII. J. Héring, *La seconde épître de saint Paul aux Corinthiens*, 1958
       IX. P. Bonnard, *L'épître de saint Paul aux Galates*:
       C. Masson, *L'épître de saint Paul aux Ephésiens*, 1953
       X. P. Bonnard, *L'épître de saint Paul aux Philippiens*:
       C. Masson, *L'épître de saint Paul aux Colossiens*, 1950
       XI. C. Masson, *Les deux épîtres de saint Paul aux Thessaloniciens*, 1957
CT   Cahiers théologiques de l'actualité protestante, publiés sous la direction de J. J. von Allmen, Neuchâtel
ET   English translation
ETR   *Etudes théologiques et religieuses*
EvTh   *Evangelische Theologie*
HNT   Handbuch zum Neuen Testament, begründet von Hans Lietzmann, Tübingen:
       8. H. Lietzmann, *An die Römer*, 4th ed., 1933
       9. H. Lietzmann and W. G. Kümmel, *An die Korinther I–II*, 4th ed., 1949
       11. M. Dibelius, *An die Thessalonicher I–II, An die Philipper*, 2nd ed., 1925
       12. M. Dibelius, *An die Kolosser, Epheser, An Philemon*, 2nd ed., 1927
       14. M. Dibelius, *Die Pastoralbriefe*, 2nd ed., 1931

Abbreviations

KEK	Kritisch-exegetischer Kommentar über das Neue Testament, begründet von H. A. W. Meyer, Göttingen:
	6. H. Windisch, *Der zweite Korintherbrief*, 9th ed., 1924
	9. E. Lohmeyer, *Briefe an die Philipper, Kolosser, Philemon*, 8th ed., 1930
NEB	New English Bible
NTS	*New Testament Studies*
RHPR	*Revue d'histoire et de philosophie religieuses*
RSV	Revised Standard Version of the Bible
RV	Revised Version of the Bible
THKNT	Theologischer Handkommentar zum Neuen Testament mit Text und Paraphrase, Leipzig:
	IX. A. Oepke, *Der Brief des Paulus an die Galater*, 1937
TLZ	*Theologische Literaturzeitung*
TWNT	*Theologisches Wörterbuch zum Neuen Testament*, begründet von Gerhard Kittel, Stuttgart
VB	*Vocabulary of the Bible*, ed. J. J. von Allmen, ET, 1956
ZNW	*Zeitschrift für die neutestamentliche Wissenschaft*
ZST	*Zeitschrift für systematische Theologie*

I

THE CHRISTIAN CONDITION

'GRAFTED into the corporeity of Christ, (the believer) loses his creatively individual existence and his natural personality. Henceforth he is only a form of manifestation of the personality of Jesus Christ, which dominates that corporeity.'[1] These words from Albert Schweitzer bring us to the first theme that confronts us: Does Paul regard life in Christ as putting an end to the human condition? Does it mean that from that moment man loses his character as a created being and become nothing more than the place where the person of Christ alone emerges? How are the reality of death and of resurrection with Christ, and the new life in him which flows from this, reflected in Christian existence? That is the kind of question that we would put to the apostle, whose experience has, by God's choice, come to us as a revelation of Christ.

It will perhaps be objected that this experience happened to Paul personally, and that we wrongly attribute to the Christian what characterizes the apostle. But does he himself draw a rigid line between the two? The exegetes are far from unanimous. Some find in his spiritual journey in the first place a suitable model for emulation. Others insist on the exceptional nature of his circumstances and commission, and indeed of the consciousness that he had of playing a privileged part in God's plan. As for the final solution, he will disclose it one day to those of his expositors who have joined him in glory (God rest their souls). Without in any way disregarding the unique role allotted by the Lord to his apostles in founding the Church, the contrast seems rather unreal. Paul never offered his place in God's plan to anyone else, either as a witness of the resurrection or as apostle to the Gentiles; they were titles that he claimed even jealously. But as

---

[1] A. Schweitzer, *The Mysticism of Paul the Apostle*, p. 125. Cf. A. Loisy: 'The Spirit of Christ becomes a collective person of which each individual is merely an element' (*Les mystères païens et le mystère chrétien*, 2nd ed., Paris, 1930, p. 256).

to his Christian life, does he not press us to become his imitators? Does he not want us to become like him—'except for these chains'? In that sense his condition as a servant of Jesus Christ is exemplary, and there is no qualitative difference between his situation and ours. To limit the relevance of his letters to the period—exceptional, but also productive—of the first Christian community would be to deprive them of all meaning for our own time.

Nowhere does the apostle reveal himself more fully than in his messages to the Corinthians—except perhaps in the opening passage of Philippians 3. The intensity of conviction imparts to this text a rhythmic movement that is remarkable.

His work is endangered by opponents who, swollen with their claims and titles, come to make mischief among the Philippians. And Paul replies by producing his, too, as he will, moreover, in II Corinthians when confronting the 'superlative apostles'. He has to go down to bed-rock to find their justification. But whereas in II Corinthians he evokes the secrets of his mystical life and his missionary labours, and in Galatians 1 he establishes the legitimacy of his apostolate, the question here is an even more fundamental one of his existence: what is his *raison d'être*? On what does he stake his adventure as a human being on earth? On what in the last resort does he base his claim? Here he is led to reveal his secret. It is significant that he often associates the words *kauchēsis* and *pepoithēsis*.[2] The first of these terms is difficult to translate. 'Boasting' hardly brings out the existential content: it is a question of knowing what we make the basis of our life, what gives it its *raison d'être* and value, in the sight of God for the believer, as well as in his own eyes and in other people's. It is the word that meets us at the beginning of Romans, when the apostle's gaze ranges over Jew and Greek to find out what is hindering them: while the latter plumes himself on his wisdom, the former has monopolized the law (given by God) which he has elaborated to make it the means of his own glorification. Paul, too, used to found his life's ultimate confidence on himself, i.e. the gifts of his own self (of his flesh). He enumerates the things by which he had up to

---

[2] Bultmann, who has not studied Heidegger in vain, has put his finger on the importance of *kauchēsis* in Pauline thought. See his *Theology of the New Testament*, p. 242f., and his article in *TWNT* III, pp. 646ff.

The Christian Condition

then been able to justify his existence: his origins, his membership of the chosen race, his status, his titles, his religious integrity, his moral uprightness, his blameless reputation, his zeal—these were his supports.

But now it is all annulled. The grace of God has put an end to his own righteousness, to bestow on him Christ's righteousness. There has now come into his life 'this mind . . . which you have in Christ Jesus' (Phil. 2.5); the events extolled by the hymn in chapter 2 find their wonderful counterpart in chapter 3.

Christ, who was divine, 'did not count equality with God a thing to be grasped, but emptied himself'; and so Paul, who was a Hebrew, of the tribe of Benjamin, considered that what he might quite legitimately have regarded as gain, honour, and glory was not a prize to be grasped, but a 'loss'. For him, Jesus made himself a servant, 'and became obedient unto death'; and now that event causes a similar reaction in the apostle's life. Paul renounces the advantages that the world could have allowed him or that he could have gained for himself; they are now 'refuse' and the word that he uses is the more violent in that it suggests his dismissing them with something of a curse—he counts them as 'refuse, in order that I may gain Christ'. Thus everything is superseded, as he declares in II Cor. 5.17, and loses all value before that single perspective in which from now onwards everything converges: to know Christ, to gain him, to be found in him. *To know him* is to know the power of his resurrection and to share his sufferings (Phil. 3.10); *to gain him* is the aim and the main effort of life (vv. 12–15); and *to be found in him* is the state which he finally attains before the supreme judgment-seat of God (11, 21). His title to glory is in Christ, and to know him is the mainspring of his being, in the full sense of a knowledge realized in love.

This knowledge appears as the discovery of the risen Lord who was crucified: 'that I may know him and the power of his resurrection, and may share his sufferings, becoming like him in his death, that if possible I may attain the resurrection from the dead.' Paul's ideas take the shape of a reversal whose double movement is most revealing. On the Damascus road Saul first met the risen Lord, who made himself known as Jesus of Nazareth who had been crucified at Golgotha, and who appeared to him as a living being who had received all power. The man who had been so sure of himself was overwhelmed; the Lord brought him forgiveness and made him completely free to serve him. Then there began the apprenticeship of the cross: the apostle found himself committed to the opposite way—the way of obedience, beginning with 'the form of a servant . . . unto death', and in his apostolic trials sharing in Jesus' sufferings, following the long road of those for whom the crucified man was Lord. Thus he was to be led by stages up to the day of resurrection when 'the Lord Jesus Christ . . . will change our lowly body to be like his glorious body, by the power which enables him even to subject all things to himself' (v. 21). Paul regards his *kenosis* as conforming to his master, and so becoming the guarantee of his own final resurrection. Thus, having been gripped by Jesus Christ, he is carried along in a sustained effort to lay hold of him, held from the outset by the one whom he is pursuing, seized by the one whom he is striving to reach.

We must never lose sight of this reversal of terms, as it bears the dialectical stamp of the apostle, and makes it possible for us to follow him faithfully. We must realize especially what separates this from the *imitatio*: Paul does not by any means try to do as Jesus did[3]—Philippians 3 does not reproduce chapter 2, but brings out the effects that the events of the cross and the resurrection have in a particular life, that of Saul of Tarsus. If we have been able to discern a striking relationship between the course taken by Jesus as extolled in the Christological hymn, and the apostle's behaviour as it appears in chapter 3, that relationship comes from God's initiative, not from that of Paul, who was 'becoming like [Christ] in his death'. The expression συμμορφίζεσθαι[4] is all the stronger in that it takes up the μορφή which was used in chapter 2 to express Christ's successively divine and servile condition. What is 'in Christ' determines what becomes of Paul; if there is a resemblance, it is not the entirely outward one of the copy to the model, but the entirely inward one of the principle to the action.[5] Henceforth the Spirit of Christ dwells in the apostle; we are

[3] On the imitation of Christ, see pp. 52ff.
[4] The verb here is passive.
[5] 'Since Christ died, in the strongest sense of the term, *for* those whom God has called, imitation can convey no more than Jesus' inward feelings, his spirit of humility, love, and sacrifice' (T. Preiss, 'Imitation et unité chez Ignace d'Antioche' in *La vie en Christ*, p. 15). Preiss quotes Luther's forceful words 'non imitatio fecit filios, sed filiatio fecit imitatores' (Weimar edition, 2, 518, 16).

The Christian Condition

'conformed to the image of his Son, in order that he might be the first-born among many brethren' (Rom. 8.29).[6] The resemblance is due not so much to attitudes as to the ties of spiritual origin; just as the ties of blood will preserve some kind of permanent indefinable family likeness between two brothers whose careers are entirely different, so there will also persist, even among the most widely differing temperaments, that deep-seated likeness between all those who have become sons of God in Jesus Christ.

As we follow in the apostle's steps, our condition now appears strangely paradoxical. Justified and yet called in question, saved and on the way to salvation, coming from death and going towards life, possessing everything and having nothing, completely free and resolutely dependent, the Christian is the man whom Luther has depicted unforgettably in *The Liberty of a Christian Man*: by faith, master of all; by love, servant of all.

All through the epistles, the guide-posts of the apostolic life show their exemplary character; the style itself bears the antithetic stamp. For instance, we may take I Cor. 4.8–13, where Paul, who outdistances the Corinthians elsewhere, checks them in their triumphal march by contrasting his own deprivation; or II Cor. 6.3–10, where he pictures in light and shadows the destiny of the preacher of the gospel, as the world reckons it and as he himself experiences it. We may think, too, of the figure used in I Corinthians 13, where the mirror reflects our present imperfect knowledge and contrasts it with the beatific face-to-face vision, whereas II Corinthians 3 allows the Christian's uncovered face already to reflect the glory of the Lord; or finally we may think of that other image, which appears twice and sums up everything —that of Jesus Christ's victorious procession traversing the reconquered world as the Roman general would celebrate his triumph in the streets of the capital. The apostle takes part in the procession, but once it will be as the captain associated with his leader's glory (II Cor. 2.14), and another time it will be well in the rear, the defeated person exhibited as 'a spectacle to the world', given over to shameful bondage or death (I Cor. 4.9). Which

---

[6] F. J. Leenhardt draws attention to the close relationship between the ideas of *form* and *glory*: 'To make conformable is to give a share in glory by allowing one to share in the Son's image' (CNT VI, on Rom. 8.29).

image are we to keep? Would not choosing mean giving away what we feel to be most genuine at the heart of the epistles?

Many explanations have been sought of these repeated contradictions: are they caused by the influence of the 'antithetic Old Testament parallelism, of popular Stoic preaching, of the "very structure of his soul", of the irreducible Gnostic dualism, of the psychological elements in his own religious experience, or of the shock of the episode on the Damascus road'?[7] All this may be part of the truth. Maurice Goguel returns continually to the unsystematic nature of Paul's thinking, where schematic lines of Jewish eschatology and what might be called the immediate data of his religious experience are intermingled.[8] Oscar Cullmann has drawn our attention to the ambiguous character of that period of the history of salvation where the future has already begun without our having as yet attained the new creation. That tension explains an ambiguous condition[9] in which what we are has not yet been manifested. We need not go over such a well-known theme again. But the theme does not of itself exhaust the paradox, as another constantly cuts across it. It was not created by the apostle's religious experiences, or by his temperament, or even by his style; these seem rather to have been shaped by an indelible imprint that they received—the original paradox of the plan of God, who mysteriously brought about the reconciliation of the world by means of the cross, Jesus Christ crucified and risen again. What Paul discerned at the heart of the Christian revelation was indeed that Christ is the crucified one; and this was brought home to him, both in the historical events within God's plan of salvation and in the Damascus encounter whose significance he perceived more clearly in the situation of man justified by Christ. At the beginning of I Corinthians Paul develops this theme in the broadest way, transposing it in turn in terms of wisdom, the interpretation of history, the Church's structure, the mystery of election, the preacher's position, and even the form of the

[7] P. Bonnard, 'Faiblesse et puissance du chrétien chez saint Paul', *ETR*, 1958, pp. 61ff.
[8] E.g. 'Le caractère à la fois actuel et futur du salut dans la théologie paulinienne', one of Goguel's last synthetic expositions of this theme, in *The Background of the New Testament and its Eschatology*, Essays in honour of C. H. Dodd, ed. W. D. Davies and D. Daube, Cambridge, 1956, pp. 322ff.
[9] One might call it 'catachronistic' as opposed to 'anachronistic'.

The Christian Condition

preaching. At last he finds himself at the beginning of his interpretation of baptism; by that sign his life will be sealed, and in that light he will understand the events that will henceforth concern him.[10]

In two noteworthy chapters of his book *The Mysticism of Paul the Apostle* Albert Schweitzer has analysed this gripping of Paul's consciousness—sufferings as a manifestation of death with Christ, and the gift of the Spirit as a manifestation of resurrection with him. Just as the Holy Spirit appears to Paul as the indisputable token of the future glory promised by his share in Christ's resurrection, so the innumerable trials that he meets one after the other along his way cannot break him; he sees in them a sure sign both that the events of Good Friday and Easter have really come home to him and that he is assuredly 'becoming like him' (Phil. 3). 'So we do not lose heart. Though our outer nature is wasting away, our inner nature is being renewed every day. For this slight momentary affliction is preparing for us an eternal weight of glory beyond all comparison' (II Cor. 4.16, 17).

With regard to this last text, and others, we must realize that the impact of the cross and resurrection transcends the old antinomy of flesh and spirit, and is not merely another example of it. We are always tempted to connect the cross with the mortification of the physical body, and the resurrection with the quickening of the soul. But on the one hand, trials and sufferings are not confined to the body; they penetrate the whole of Paul's being; they arise not only from his earthly condition, but more often from his belonging to Jesus Christ. The outward man, of

[10] In a recent work, *A New Quest of the Historical Jesus* (Studies in Biblical Theology 25), 1959, J. M. Robinson stresses how certain passages in which Paul dialectically describes his condition bear the mark of the Christological confessions that express the sequence of the Lord's abasement and elevation (thus I Cor. 15.3–5; Phil. 2.5–11; Gal. 4.4–5; Rom. 1.3–4, etc.). The author shows that side by side with the expressions drawn from his own experience, Paul tends to use those that come from the kerygma, so much so that there sometimes ceases to be any obvious dividing line between what we might call autobiographical elements and preaching. The existential interpretation of the kerygma and the kerygmatic interpretation of existence merge, as they do in the Gospels. Moreover, they unite in a remarkable way with Jesus' conception of life, as it appears to us from his preaching. J. Baruzi had noticed earlier the structural analogy between the hymn of Phil. 2 and the text of II Cor. 12, Paul interpreting his deepest mystical experience in the light of the early Church's 'chorale' (cf. *Création religieuse et pensée contemplative* I, pp. 50ff.). 'It is impossible to make out', Baruzi writes, 'where the theological construction begins, at what point it takes over from the recollection the inward progress that was part of his life and is incommensurate with any other.'

whose destruction they are evidence, is the old man κατὰ σάρκα On the other hand, the resurrection of Jesus, as we see from the apostle's hope with regard to his own body, does not affect his spirit only; the πνεῦμα is at work here and now in his body, which is its temple, and the life of Jesus is 'manifested in [his] mortal flesh' (II Cor. 4.10, 11).[11] Thus death and resurrection with Christ do not act as if on two parallel planes; the repercussions meet and intermingle in such a way as to give the Christian's condition that paradoxical character that can be adequately understood only by the discerning power of the Spirit.

We must note that, in the long run, they do not end in the total mortification of the old Adam (except in physical death, which indeed can be very brutal), nor in a final transfiguration into what is new. Paul thinks of his life as 'straining forward to what lies ahead', rather than as a gradual ascent towards the eternal peaks. However his thought may have evolved with regard to the time of the parousia, he never counted on anything but the Lord's coming in glory to effect the final transformation of his being.[12] In this sense we cannot speak of the *progress* of life in Christ. Yet to many people the text of II Cor. 4.16, which we have just quoted, has seemed to be one of the assertions least open to question. To quote H. Lietzmann: 'The inward being is the kernel of the new creature, which goes on developing continuously'; or J. Héring: 'The inward being is the new Adam who grows mysteriously until the moment of his revelation.'[13]

Can it be that Paul had in mind a continuous development here? No; he had in mind the renewing of divine grace that allowed

---

[11] Cf. O. Cullmann, 'La délivrance anticipée du corps humain d'après le Nouveau Testament', in *Hommage et reconnaissance à Karl Barth* (CT, Hors-Série 2), 1946, p. 31.

[12] It seems very likely that Paul had at first thought of the Christian's death as something abnormal. He expected the parousia before the end of his generation, and Christians were to be transfigured on the Lord's appearance. 'The doctrine of a resurrection after death is certainly an innovation imposed by the brutal fact of the delay of the parousia and the numerous deaths in the Church' (J. Héring, *Royaume de Dieu*, p. 242, referring to Albert Schweitzer, *Mysticism*, p. 91). But even there, the definitive transfiguration is achieved, not by evolution, but by the Lord's coming in glory.

[13] H. Lietzmann, HNT 9, *ad loc.*; J. Héring, CNT VIII, *ad loc.* Héring, moreover, has very happily outlined the idea (often a confused one) of the *inward being*; not an anthropological dimension that has to be added to the already complex assemblage of body, flesh, soul, spirit, etc., but a *soteriological* category: it is the germ of the future man, which is as yet invisible and will be revealed at the last. It assures the *continuity of consciousness* between the two states. Cf. the *Royaume de Dieu*, p. 185 n. 2, and CNT VII, p. 148.

The Christian Condition

him to go forward towards the time when he would take possession of the promised inheritance, 'an eternal weight of glory beyond all comparison' (II Cor. 4.17).[14] The creature who is still tied by the bonds of the flesh to this passing world grows old and wrinkled and decays; but, as he already belongs to the world that is to come, he receives from it the fulness of youth that is the opposite of that which fades day by day, one that goes not from life to death but from death to life.

Nor does the apostle seem to foresee any gradual transformation when he writes, a little earlier, 'We . . . are being changed into his likeness from one degree of glory to another' (II Cor. 3.18). Our calling has conformed us to the image of Christ (Rom. 8.28, 29),[15] so that one day that image should be fully revealed in us. Meanwhile the Christian life moves on, born of the initial glory (that of the preaching of the gospel which has confronted us face to face and gives 'the dispensation of the Spirit' [II Cor. 3.9] its incomparable greatness), and going on to meet the final, everlasting glory, that of the Kingdom.[16] So we cannot agree unreservedly with Baruzi when he writes, 'The essence of Paul's mysticism and dialectic is to be sought in an intimate transmutation of the body in contact with the *pneuma*.'[17] In so far as these words suggest a process of spiritualization, they depart from

---

[14] In this sense cf. H. Windisch, KEK 6, *ad loc*. He quotes the strange rabbinical declaration: 'Every night the devout man entrusts the care of his soul to God, and in the morning he receives it again into his body, as a new creation . . .' It is quite obvious that the *inward being* cannot be identified with this soul, and that our sleep at night does not interrupt our belonging to Christ.

[15] We know the importance of the idea of *image*, which must be stripped of its present formal meaning, so that we can give it back the vigour and transforming power that it has in Scripture, where it implies such conformity to the original as to show it in its entirety. Thus it can be applied to Jesus only in proportion as we have seen in him the heavenly Man, the second Adam. The Old Testament never referred to the text of Genesis to identify anyone or anything with the *imago Dei*; that is an object of hope, and no one can see it or venture to identify it (see Masson, CNT X, on Col. 1.15). Plato's boldness was to discover it in the *cosmos*, while Paul's was to discover it (as 'folly') in the crucified Lord! To the believer, it expresses the relative character of the new creature in relation to Christ, the real Adam, who remains God's image *par excellence*; and it equally implies the reality of forgiveness, a proximity that is henceforth both possible and immediate, where nothing can now separate or come between the Lord and his creation.

[16] 'From one degree of glory to another'; there is an analogous turn of speech in Rom. 1.17: 'For in [the gospel] the righteousness of God is revealed ἐκ πίστεως εἰς πίστιν'. Kittel has given one of the best interpretations of this passage, because he has rightly put it in the light of the context of II Corinthians, that is, of the ministry of the gospel (cf. *TWNT* II, p. 254).

[17] J. Baruzi, *Création religieuse* I, p. 55.

authentic Paulinism; but if the author wishes them to imply that the power of the Spirit takes possession of the individual, including his body, as of the community, then they lead to it.

We noted, a moment ago, that the *inward* man belongs to soteriological categories, and is not derived from biology. In becoming the temple of the Spirit, the individual has not secured some privilege of transmutation that would enable him to withdraw from his human condition and go on ahead of it. He remains subject to the mysterious rhythm of the history of salvation. He goes at its pace. He is bound up with it. The spirituality of the Exodus, the theology of God's people *en route* for the promised Kingdom, remains the necessary axis of the apostle's vision, and in this he is in line with the general body of Scripture.[18] Both his conception of the Church and his consciousness of our condition here and now are characterized by this. The 'religious' life follows a curve of withdrawal, individualization, and inwardness; with Paul, the incomparable movement of the Christian life seems to soar away towards outward things, towards other people, towards communication. The one rises, the other goes forward and 'presses on towards the goal'.

But, it will be objected, are there not a number of passages that open out a perspective of *growth*? Did not Paul use the various stages of existence to describe the Christian condition? 'The divine life of which the gospel speaks is dynamic; . . . it begins with birth as physical life does, and everything is born in order to grow. That is as true on the spiritual as on the biological plane. Believers, who are the newly born of the Spirit, are at first "babes in Christ", says St Paul (I Cor. 3.1). They have to grow if they are to become "mature" (I Cor. 2.6) and reach "the measure of the stature of the fulness of Christ" (Eph. 4.13; Col. 1.28). . . .'[19] Who would deny this dynamism? Yet the apostle seems to be unaware of, or at any rate to avoid, this image of birth. When he talks about the origins of the new life, as in Rom. 6.3ff., he hardly pauses on the road of development, but sets off at once on that of obedience. Romans 8 goes on to suggest the full blossoming of that life; but all its continuity and sequence are directed towards God, so to speak, much more than towards

---

[18] We would refer to L. Cerfaux, *The Church in the Theology of St Paul* (ET, 1959).
[19] P. H. Menoud's essay in *L'homme face à la mort*, Neuchâtel, 1952, p. 182.

The Christian Condition

man, especially in the *ordo salutis* developed in verses 28-30—the first-born Son among many brethren who follow his leading from predestination to calling, from calling to justification, from justification to glory. These stages depend not on psychology but on the divine initiative.

There is no falser interpretation of Paulinism than that of the commentators—all too numerous—who have, as it were, regarded the apostle as static from the moment of his conversion; they have remained on the threshold, and have caught no glimpse of the realism with which, starting with justification by faith, he realized that he was involved in a new existence that implied a transformation of his whole being. But with the ideas of spiritual germ, new birth, and indeed growth, we are bordering on Hellenistic territory, recognizable in particular by the idea of a redemption that proceeds by degrees of initiation. It is no use looking for their roots in the Old Testament. Even when he used biological figures of speech, the apostle never went over entirely to that 'vital' current. The stages on life's way are not εἰς Χριστόν, but ἐν Χριστῷ. The apostle's toil does not suggest to believers that they are to climb a mystical ladder, but rather that they are to make their way along the road to maturity, i.e. towards complete liberation from this world's hold over them, so that they may realize what they already are. This realization can be completed only by Christ's being perfectly formed in us, as in the apostle's struggles, his travails, in pain and joy, over Corinth, Galatia, and Colossae. The community and the Christian have attained their majority because the living person of Christ has freed himself from instruction, as also from inward searchings and arguments, to assert himself henceforth with authority, both in them and through them.[20]

The idea of growth presupposes that the movement of life, according to the natural order, springs from a peculiar impulse, that of procreation and birth, and that the creature then develops as a result of the initial propulsive force. There is no doubt that the Christian, too, when he is converted, receives the dynamic strength, the continually new impulse of the *pneuma* that confers

---

[20] It should be remembered that Gal. 4.19 concerns the Church before it refers to the individual. The 'in you' *(ἐν ὑμῖν)* keeps its complementary meaning of 'among you' and 'within you'.

on him a unique impetus. But this is not the last words about Paul's thought. We have already noticed the very close analysis that J. Dupont has applied to the beginning of II Corinthians 5.[21] The 'vital' thrust is there, as it were, telescoped by another force that meets it head on, and in consequence the text keeps its highly intricate character, in which Père Dupont unravels mystical Hellenistic elements and apocalyptic traces. The idea of birth and life, which the apostle can borrow as easily from comparisons of natural order as from the religious terminology of mysteries, and the idea of life proceeding 'from the initial glory', meet the opposite movement, the 'apocalyptic' force which proceeds 'from the final glory' (cf. II Cor. 3.18). The natural law of *source* comes to combine with a specific spiritual law of *attraction*; the Christian life gets its dynamism no less from its *end* than from its origin, from what is before it than from what is behind it.[22] Thus the Kingdom that is to come determines our condition, in Christ. We have moved into the field of attraction which the 'weight' of future glory exerts on the world through the Spirit; it is not unreasonable to associate the biblical idea of *glory* with the image of a magnetic mass that is *already* in action, at a distance and without having as yet been fully revealed, and bringing out features of history that are mysterious and at present inexplicable. If we leave out eschatological considerations, we reduce Paul's dynamism simply to a doctrine of evolution. Does not the joy of a life that does not decline but is renewed from day to day arise from the productive union of the animating force that comes from the cross, through the Spirit, and the force that is already being given out, through the same Spirit, by the Lord who is 'near'?

It would be right to interpret similarly Paul's repeated and pressing exhortations to a renewing of the mind. Not in the sense of *gnosis*, where knowledge leads to life—here it is life that leads to knowledge. Christians, as God's adopted children, are urged by their apostolic teacher not to stagnate in the age of childhood, but to go forward without slackening towards the adulthood that

---

[21] See *En Christ*, pp. 39-40. Cf. Jacques Dupont, $\Sigma YN\ XPI\Sigma T\Omega I$. *L'union avec le Christ suivant saint Paul* I.

[22] God's work is not tied down by the laws of the natural order. Lohmeyer reminds us of Eckhardt's words: 'Nature makes the man from the child, and the hen from the egg. God makes the man before the child, and the hen before the egg' (KEK 9, on Col. 1.6).

The Christian Condition

exercises spiritual insight and is characterized by 'all wisdom'.[23] Adam tried to snatch at the knowledge of good and evil; the *whole man* receives it, thanks to the *renewing of the mind* which allows him to judge for himself of what is seemly.[24]

But there again, we shall never rise to complete success. Paul indeed goes so far as to speak of the τέλειοι (Phil. 3.15); but at that very moment he has remembered that he has 'not . . . already obtained this' (3.12). The paradox of our condition is shown again, and could hardly be better expressed. Perfection embraces the whole, and implies a completeness never achieved by *homo viator* (I Cor. 13.10). The undeniable references to 'perfect'[25] that have aroused so many arguments cannot be generalized; however contradictory it may appear, these expressions are only relative to a point reached, a given community, a particular object. This perfection, in fact, will never become individual; it is achieved only in community.[26]

Paul does not hesitate to speak of the *progress* of faith (Phil. 1.25; II Cor. 10.15; II Thess. 1.3) and of love (I Thess. 3.12; Phil. 1.9), but it is mainly in the sense of mutual strengthening and common

---

[23] 'If Paul contrasts childhood and maturity, it is not so as to depreciate childhood, but to insist on the movement by which it develops beyond childhood': M. Philibert, in a very suggestive study (*Une foi adulte pour le temps présent*, Strasbourg, 1962), examines in detail what the continual making of a Christian must consist of. He quotes an impressive number of texts that give apostolic affirmations and exhortations: on the development of the mind (Phil. 1.9; Rom. 12.2; I Cor. 3.1-2; 13.11; 14.20 . . .); on the mature man's judgment (I Cor. 2.5; 5.12-13; 6.2-3; 10.15; 11.13, 28-31; II Cor. 13.5; Gal. 6.4; Rom. 16.17; Eph. 4.23; 5.10, 15, 17; Col. 4.5).

[24] We must be careful not to make this mental liberation a merely individual matter; it is inseparable from the evolution of the community: 'No one goes forward' writes M. Philibert, 'unless he is drawn along by some and draws others along with him.'

[25] Sometimes 'mature' in the RSV.

[26] The most controversial texts are those of I Cor. 2, where Reitzenstein found the clearest indication that the apostle was influenced by mysteries. As early as 1918 this point of view was refuted by K. Deissner (*Paul und die Mystik seiner Zeit*, Leipzig, 1918).

We shall not take part in the discussion, except to recall the internal coherence of the Pauline terminology, which closely connects God's plan, wisdom, management, mystery, insight, knowledge, and perfection. It is also as well to emphasize the meaning of *teleios* in the LXX: the word, which is rather rare, means 'wholly' (e.g. I Kings 11.4—Solomon's heart is divided, and no longer perfect; and similarly Deut. 18.13: 'You shall be blameless' [i.e. you shall belong perfectly, without restriction] 'before the Lord your God.'

We do not think one can make of Paul's *teleioi* a separate class of Christians in the sense understood by the Qumran community, for example, with its *rabbim*, or even by our churches, when they speak of active or 'committed' members.

We shall deal later with Col. 1.28. Its terms have a markedly sacrifical meaning.

Christianity According to Paul

perseverance; it is the counterpoint accompanying the plainsong. Here the plainsong, namely the gospel, is the only reality whose progress the apostle, in the last resort, acknowledges. He has taken part with the Philippians in its advance (Phil. 1.5).[27] It is certainly not controlled by missionary success or failure; there is revealed in it a power of extensive and intensive growth that constitutes the sinews of history, and for which the apostle, as an amazed onlooker, can give thanks; the believers rise up as the landmarks of the gospel's progress through the world, and its power is shown in their increasing faith and love. The apostolic preaching helps the gospel onwards, and exhortation watches over the development of its fruits: become then, in the Lord, what you are in Christ![28]

One objection remains to be met, and it concerns passages taken from Ephesians or Colossians. We shall have occasion to come back to the characteristics of these letters, in which the dimensions seem to be spatial rather than temporal. The theology of the body has precedence over that of God's people, as, by the same token, growth has over the march forward. The approach of salvation, 'nearer to us now than when we first believed' (Rom. 13.11), is replaced by growth upwards towards 'Christ, the Head' (see Col. 2.19; Eph. 2.21; 4.15, etc.). This is not the place to discuss these texts (to which we shall return in ch. IV), except to emphasize that they once again point to the churchly dimension of 'the stature of the fulness of Christ' (Eph. 4.13), a stature reached thanks to mutual participation in Christ's love 'which binds everything together in perfect harmony' (Col. 3.14). Real growth (building up) is a growth of communion and of communication, and the complete image is realized in the new man that we are to become in him.

But it would not do to set up these two letters in opposition to the others. The strength of such texts as Col. 3.9–12, or its parallel Eph. 4.24, which were used as a starting-point of a famous lecture by Karl Barth on 'The reality of the new man', is in their ethical tone, in the assertion of a radical break with previous morals and conduct, and the surprising emergence of a new being

---

[27] Cf. Acts 6.7: 'And the word of God increased.'
[28] We find here the connections that exegesis has shown between ἐν Χριστῷ and ἐν κυρίῳ.

The Christian Condition

into which we are to be changed, having put on, in Christ, kindness, humility, meekness, and patience.[29]

Two complementary lines meet—that of the theology of the body, tending to develop organic images of growth, and that which comes from the theme of God's people, from the eschatological impulse to restore everything to unceasing dependence on him who is coming (Phil. 3.20). The vital current coming down, and that first movement going up, as it were, under the pressure of the end of things, meet and intermingle, sometimes apparently causing conflicting eddies, but uniting to remind us continually of the unlimited extent of God's sovereignty.

Thus, as far as his present condition is concerned, Paul depends entirely on another. He is not certain of going on to greater discoveries; it may well be that he will undergo increasing deprivation. 'What does it matter,' he exclaims, 'seeing that Christ is proclaimed, and that, now as always, he will be honoured in my body, whether by life or by death!' (Phil. 1.18–20). Up hill and down dale, by the bitter waters of Marah and the heights of Sinai, the miraculous hours at the Red Sea and the burning temptations of the wilderness of Sin, on the Damascus road, on the first missions, amid the joys of Macedonia and the trials of Ephesus, in the heights of the third heaven and at the point of despair even of life, God takes his people onward, as he takes his apostle. Their only care is to render faithful obedience at every stage of the journey. They go on, following the one whom they love, from day to day, from town to town, from joy to joy, from trial to trial, from Eucharist to Eucharist. . . .

Perhaps we may be allowed to summarize these features in a

---

[29] Thus Behm in *TWNT* III, p. 454. We know that the expression 'new man' is one of the most difficult in Pauline terminology, whatever origin we give it. Sometimes it obviously refers to the second Adam, to be identified with Christ (Eph. 2.15), as is suggested by ὅπου (Col. 3.11) (the new man *where* there is now neither Greek nor Jew—that is the only way to give the force of the ὅπου). Sometimes it is something like the 'inward man' (cf. Eph. 4.24), and this seems to be indicated by 'renewed in the spirit of your minds'. One can hardly fail to recall the other biblical expressions, such as 'servant of the Lord', 'Son of man', where exegesis has hesitated in the same way between the personal and the collective.

On the moral and practical character of the word, compare Phil. 1.9 with Philemon 6; and see Bultmann, *TWNT* I, p. 707.

picture whose aptness may excuse its banality.[30] The Christian condition, as we see it here in outline, may be compared to a mountain climb. The Kingdom is indeed an inaccessible summit, an unconquered rock-face which none of those who attempted it could scale—neither the Greeks by their own methods, nor the Jews using the legal technique (and its rope ladders). Jesus Christ in his turn appeared, as a servant. With no vestige of presumption or self-glorification, he opened the way by carrying out a breathtaking 'first performance'. He reveals himself as the victor. He was thought to be irretrievably lost, condemned to death, nailed to a cross, and now he appears on high, alive. And he calls the others to come the way that he himself has been: the moment has come for those who have been 'seized' by him to press forward.

To imitate him would mean that, as Jesus has led the way, believers have only to watch his actions and movements—or to read the textbook—so as to try, with more or less success, to travel the way that he did. Another temptation would be to think that, as Jesus has overcome the rock-face *for me*, I have already reached the objective, and really have nothing more to do than to let myself be hoisted up like a sack at the end of a rope—or even that I have no need to trouble about anything, as he has done it all! No, the fact that he has arrived is precisely the reason for our being in action, just as the mountaineers roped together follow the guide. That is to say, he is *in front*; the difficult places where we should be certain to come to grief in the face of insurmountable obstacles and overhanging rocks, and death itself—that last chasm where we should sway hopelessly in space—he has faced them and triumphed over them alone, leading the way, with no possibility of help or support from anyone, risking death for us all. And now that he has forced the key positions and has reached the summit, even though for the moment he is hidden from me by the rock-face that I still have to climb, he *ensures* my safety and that of my companions, at every step, with the rope. We go forward because he has conquered. We share here and now in his sufferings and in the difficulties that he encountered,

---

[30] We have recently found one more variation in the introduction to Eduard Schweizer's *Erniedrigung und Erhöhung*, in a form that is perhaps less adapted to our theme. It is hardly necessary to emphasize, after what has been said above, that the main point of the picture is not some spiritual ascent. As someone has said, the 'Alpine club' mentality has worked havoc in the ranks of the pietists.

by which we already know that we are saved. We, too, have to bear thirst, scorching sun and icy hail; but we have this hope of reaching the final goal. People do not all meet the same conditions, of course; some encounter storms, others ideal weather; but everyone has his trials, his self-denials, and his responsibilities towards others. There will be times when one has to do as he did in a physical sense. But the efforts are not futile, nor is the course hypothetical: he is there, quite close, urging us on to victory, to the joy of reunion up there, and to what is already within his view, the vast horizon from the summit. He is up there; I can only see the rope hanging down, and I go on by faith, in fellowship with my fellow climbers, for we help each other as we go.

II

COMMUNION WITH CHRIST

Thus the Christian condition comes solely from Christ. But it would be a mistake to reduce that dependence to historical determination, or to existential conformity, or to dogmatic assertion. In the epistles Christ's imprint has the indelible character of communion of life and love. No doubt 'mysticism' has been one of the most misused words, and we have pointed out its dangers and ambiguities; but it will not do to reject it entirely, in so far as it reveals the bond that united the apostle and his Lord, and which, if taken away, leaves the epistles like an empty shell. Everyone knows the great texts where that fervent communion is passionately revealed, even if others, perhaps less famous, may take us closer to the apostle's heart.

We shall not be able to see clearly, in all its depth, the personal relationship with Christ unless we allow for its triple dimension, which has already appeared so clearly; it springs from the relationship that Jesus Christ has formed with us; it is lit up by the relationship that will be made plain in the glory of the Kingdom; and it is nourished by his living presence.[1] If we wanted to recover the original expressions, we should have to say in succession 'dead and raised with Christ' (a mysticism of baptism), 'with Christ in glory' (a mysticism of waiting), and (simultaneously) 'with Christ in God'[2] and 'Christ in us'. The first gives us the past, the second the future, and the third the present. If it may sometimes be an artificial distinction, it is more dangerous to confuse them and thereby to forget one of the dimensions without which everything is distorted.

1. UNION WITH CHRIST

Personal relationship with Christ is not an immediate relationship. It comes through the sacrament, because it comes across

---

[1] See *En Christ*, ch. IV.

[2] We must remember that 'with Christ in glory' describes our future sharing in the Kingdom, after the parousia; 'with Christ in God' describes one of the results of baptism.

Communion with Christ

history. It results from events that took place at the beginning of our era, events that concerned the person of this Jesus, a poor Jew who went from village to village doing good, who died on a wooden cross, and who, his disciples asserted, was raised from the dead. That existence might of itself stand out in history through the image, the being, the words, and the actions of that man among men. And yet the only way that we can understand its influence on our destiny is through memory or example, unless we accept the apostles' testimony, which is that God in his sovereignty intervened to make known his righteousness, i.e. to make good the claim of his creative plan, and to reconcile the world to himself: 'God shows his love for us in that while we were yet sinners Christ died for us' (Rom. 5.8).

Not only Jesus' sufferings, his temptations, agony and death, but also his joys, his answered prayers, his miracles and victories, are thus given their full significance, not by their grand, heroic, universal character (one might add to the description), but by God's decree: the divine grace takes completely, in order to *give* it, that life which is so completely offered up that it has nothing private to itself—takes it away from what might have permanently limited it to itself, its individual, ephemeral, and contingent character. God chooses to confine to the coming of him whom he reveals as the second Adam the explicit value set out in Rom. 5: Adam and Jesus Christ incarnate the two human natures, or, if we like, human nature in its twofold destiny—rebellion and obedience, condemnation and justification, death and life, defeat and victory, isolation and communion. As soon as the apostle goes on from that 'one man's act of righteousness' to its results, he is inevitably led, in chapter 6, to the question of baptism; here the paths—Christ's and mine—converge. Jesus Christ died and was raised again for us, and so we, dead and raised again with him, are personally affected by everything that concerns him.

We met these basic texts when we studied the expression 'with Christ';[3] and we note the dissymetry that gives all the force of a completed action to the fact of being 'buried with him', but on the other hand orients the fact of 'living with him' towards a future full of promise and charged with ethical content, the apostle leaving aside both magic and symbolism. Baptism and the

[3] See *En Christ*, pp. 38ff.

cross originate in a similar initiative:[4] just as Jesus has identified himself with us, 'being born in the likeness of men' (Phil. 2.7), so we have become 'united with him in a death like his' (Rom. 6.5). The power to effect this conformation is given equally to the coming in the flesh and to baptism, both of which create a bond of the same quality, from him to us and from us to him.

Faith therefore takes the decisive step of recognizing in every action of Jesus of Nazareth an action that concerns us personally. No single moment of his life is unimportant to us, and no word of his without an echo, since, having come to *serve*, he is given to us. This offering of Christ to us is the work of the Spirit, and the Lord's Supper, in its turn, testifies to it in a wonderful way. His life, offered and received, becomes ours. In the waters of Jordan, in the wilderness of Judea, under the olive-trees of Gethsemane, the last words were said about my baptism, my temptations, my prayers. The righteousness that I have is no longer mine; my eternal destiny is decided by the judgment given at Golgotha, and my future depends neither on my successes nor on my failures; in Christ I benefit by the only success that exists in the world—that of Easter: 'Once for all, we have passed from death to life.' The closely woven fabric of days and hours, of actions and thoughts that form the web of life and are the stuff of its daily reality, no longer contains either its secret or its ending; it was when the cross was set up about the year 30 that issue was joined with death, and the paschal dawn that coloured the Jerusalem sky on a day of unleavened bread was the dawn of my life. I die in his death; I am raised in his resurrection; I am righteous in his righteousness, sanctified in his sanctity, chosen in his election. I live in his life: 'For me to live is Christ' (Phil. 1.21).

Even so, the road has not ended. We have known those things that lie ahead, and their meaning: we go forward by faith and not by sight, waiting for the new creation. In our course, as yet unfinished, one certainty remains; no human situation is foreign to our Lord, and, in that sense, sin no longer has any power over us.

---

[4] F. J. Leenhardt has rightly insisted on the place held by the Jewish sacrificial doctrine in Paul's explanation of baptism (CNT VI, on Rom. 6.3, 4). We must never separate redemption from the new creation. It is T. Preiss's merit to have united in his 'juridical mysticism' what had wrongly been contrasted—life in Christ and justification by faith.

Communion with Christ

Christ has walked along our human way, and he goes before us. Where could we go lower than he has gone? Where could we climb higher than he has been raised? He has taken on himself the unforeseeable contingencies of our free and personal adventure. In the worst extremity he anticipates us, because he himself has gone down to the lowest depth, that of the complete absence of God. He became 'a curse for us', and our hell itself belongs to him. No situation, therefore, will be able to break up this new life by tearing us away from the Father's love—neither the past nor the future, neither height nor depth, neither heavenly power nor earthly. We are 'united with him' (Rom. 6.5); that is the irrevocable *judgment* of him who destined us to be conformed to the image of his Son.

2. WAITING FOR CHRIST

The study of the expression 'with Christ' has revealed to us another aspect of union with the Lord—one that will be unfolded in the future glory of the Kingdom. 'With Christ', we said, was the second pillar on which life *in Christo* rests and is built up, like an arch, between the resurrection and the parousia. We shall not try here to discuss the blessed life opened to us through baptism, that 'far better' life that made the apostle Paul wish so eagerly for his 'departure'; such a study has, in fact, already been made.[5] We now propose rather to look for the bearing of that hope on our present relationship to Jesus Christ.

The 'theologies of glory' which stress only the present follow a blind alley: by anticipating the stages in the history of salvation, they put before the believer the impossible obligation of becoming in himself what he is in Christ.[6] 'The prize of the high calling' has

---

[5] See J. Dupont, *L'union avec le Christ*. . . .

[6] There is a striking example in Schweitzer's *Mysticism*. For him mysticism, anticipating time, goes forward into the life to come. He regards it as the crowning of the apostle's faith, but he loses sight of the, as yet, equivocal nature of our condition. We have seen that, according to Schweitzer, we have already left our mortal body to clothe ourselves in the glorious body: 'For those who have died and risen again the flesh and sin have been completely done away with. . . . The limitations of the natural existence no longer apply to them.' But when we go on to ethical problems we have to drop any expressions of triumph. To make his mysticism agree with everyday experience, Schweitzer has recourse to will and duty: 'The believer, by his will, should progressively make into a reality his death to the flesh and sin, and his being ruled in his thinking and acting by the Spirit's new principles of life' (p. 301). This mysticism asserts itself with no direct hold on material things; it is on a par with law and morality. It does not now beget ethics as in Paul's dialectic.

Christianity According to Paul

not yet been carried off; we are on the way to the final recovery of our salvation on which our hopes are centred here below.

Paul's hope is expressed through two hymns that people have often tried to contrast or to spread out in time, but which are found at the same time in the same letter. Paul saw no contradiction in them; he did not hesitate to make use of anything to express his deepest spiritual experience. The source of one of these hymns is mystical, and of the other apocalyptic. The latter rises in Hebraic language, 'From heaven we await a Saviour, our Lord Jesus Christ, who will change our lowly body to be like his glorious body. (Phil. 3.21), while the former adopts a more Hellenistic strain, 'My desire is to depart and be with Christ' (1.23). This waiting, bound up with the final accomplishment of God's plan, and this desire, bound up with the completion of the earthly course, have for Paul the same object: to overcome the resistance that time and bodily existence still offer to complete communion with his Lord, whose presence is revealed at the heart of an absence that the apostle at times feels poignantly. He lives in the hope of this meeting—a meeting either after death, still partial and provisional, but even so 'far better'; or after the parousia, in the universal fulfilment of salvation.[7] J. Dupont thinks that, in the apocalyptic perspective, the phrase 'to be with the Lord' does not indicate an aspiration 'towards the final blossoming of a friendship between the believers and their Lord', but rather the hope of the Kingdom's blessedness and glory.[8] He is right to stress the features borrowed by the Pauline hope from the traditional picture in the thought of Israel; but what would that blessedness and glory be to Paul unless he found at the centre the one who is its source? What would the eschatological feast be if Christ were not there to preside over it?

The expectation therefore has the twofold effect of casting shadow as well as light on our communion with Christ:

(*a*) The more the apostle extols the fulness of the reality that he has seen from afar, when we shall know as we have been known, and love as we have been loved, when we are face to face with glory, the greater prominence he gives to the distance that

---

[7] As J. Héring well puts it, 'The apostle renounced eschatological impatience by giving himself up to Christ from now onward' (*Le Royaume de Dieu*, p. 242).
[8] J. Dupont, *L'union avec le Christ* . . ., pp. 99ff.

Communion with Christ

still separates us from it. It seems that just when he allows his cries of triumph to break out he hastens to apply the corrective ('the eschatological reservation', as it has been called), not to devalue the assurance of salvation, but to give it precision; not to turn his flock away, but to make sure of not misleading them. After talking about gaining Christ and being found in him (Phil. 3.8f.) Paul at once adds, 'Not that I have already obtained [the prize].' When he has exclaimed, 'For all things are yours . . . the world or life or death . . .' he goes on, with pained irony, 'Already you are filled. Already you have become rich. Without us you have become kings' (I Cor. 4.8). 'I do not run aimlessly,' he says elsewhere, '. . . . I pommel my body and subdue it, lest after preaching to others I myself should be disqualified' (I Cor. 9.26f.). Or again, 'If anyone imagines that he knows something, he does not yet know as he ought to know' (I Cor. 8.2); and finally 'We know that while we are at home in the body we are away from the Lord' (II Cor. 5.6).

Thus the believer cannot presume on any *security* before God or man. Communion with Christ does not take him out of his human condition; it does not enrich him—on the contrary, it deprives him. He believes without touching, he loves without seeing, he lives *in Christo* away from Christ. Jesus has come to us in so far as he (and in fact, only he) has experienced the absence of God. We, too, cannot escape the trial of our faith, and it is precisely in this *kenosis* that life in Christ, far from separating us by some overwhelming privilege, puts us fairly and squarely with a humanity that is separated from and at the same time called by God; what the Christian knows is not the satisfaction of ownership that would make him intolerable to other people, but the thirst that he can share with everyone.

In the poverty of one who is not yet master of his inheritance, the fellow heir with Christ awaits the hour. At the heart of a creation that groans earnestly but unconsciously, he gives these inarticulate cries the fervour of a prayer, because he has received a guarantee of the Spirit and because Christ lives in him; he knows who is coming. The Lord's Supper illustrates very well our present destitution. The more the Lord feeds us, the hungrier we are; and when he shows us his presence there, we can only beg him to put a term to his absence: *maranatha*!

(*b*) But these shadows are, as it were, only cast by the light of expectation. Christ in us, the hope of glory! *Maranatha* is also the joyful cry of the Church, thrilled with gladness at the movement of the eucharistic feast. Jesus is neither behind nor beyond, but in front, close at hand, the one who is coming; and we are going to meet him.[9] Amid uncertainties and contradictory views, that is the one point beyond dispute. The Lord's life among this people represents no resurgence of the past; it is the advance signal for the glorious assembly that is the rallying-point of the Church on its forward march.

The presence of Christ, like the gift of the Spirit, of which it is the fruit, is the pledge—no more than a pledge—received here of the world to come and of life in the Kingdom. It enables us to see —vaguely, so that our longing for it may be aroused—the face-to-face meeting; and by teaching us to live, it gives us an inkling of what the fulness of love will be. The Master who is coming is the one in whom we have believed and lived. No good gift of God is any longer something transitory: now that it is in Christ it already partakes of this coming, and thus the new life appears as a continual invitation to go further, reminding us of what we have not yet received, the inheritance that is being kept for us in heaven. Thus the Christian life is firmly oriented, not only towards what is new and unforeseeable, but also towards what is known and loved in the expected parousia. We have the ratification of this in the Lord's Supper, which tells us of the Lord's death till he returns; the bread and wine are at once gifts of his presence and tokens of his absence, and foreshadow a feast whose unutterable happiness we can only conjecture.

This is where we must tell of the *joy* of life in Christ, that messianic exultation that springs, not from possession, but from trembling expectation, the very joy of the beatitudes. Its hands are empty, but it is on the road to abundance. And indeed, the opposite to joy would be to think that everything is already ours, and that salvation has reached its final dimensions. 'If in this life only we have hoped in Christ, we are of all men most to be pitied. But in fact Christ has been raised from the dead, the first fruits of those who have fallen asleep' (I Cor. 15.19f.). How can we enter

---

[9] On the procession going to meet the Lord, see again J. Dupont, *op. cit.*, pp. 64–73.

Communion with Christ

into joy as long as the whole being is not unreservedly involved? And as long as others are left out? How could eternal happiness be enjoyed as long as one of the Father's children was absent from the roll-call? 'Without having seen him you love him; though you do not now see him you believe in him and rejoice with unutterable and exalted joy' (I Peter 1.8).

3. CHRIST'S PRESENCE

In studying the expression 'with Christ' we have seen the formation of two guiding lines that came from baptism: the one that we see in the great epistles, and the other that is the original contribution of Ephesians-Colossians; the former, from sharing in Christ's death, opening out on the perspective of a new life to be lived in obedience, and the latter already launching out into the resurrection. The latter draws us upward and makes us 'sit with him in the heavenly places' (Eph. 2.6); the former draws *him* into *our* earthly wanderings. Both derive from the connecting-point of baptism; but whereas the latter stresses the bond from us to him— our being raised again with him—the former stresses the bond from him to us and brings it right into our history and histories, in what takes place here below till he comes.[10] The latter is expressed in the life 'hid with Christ in God' (Col. 3.3), the other in the hidden life manifested by Christ in us. We do not know which formulation came first,[11] but we do know that each is necessary to the other, since together they form the twofold aspect, the complementary expression of the present relationship that unites with Christ.

(*a*) *The life hidden with Christ in God*

'If then you have been raised with Christ, seek the things that are above, where Christ is, seated at the right hand of God. . . .'

---

[10] We may say that one is transcendent and the other immanent—but those philosophical terms . . . ! It is of more interest to recall that one was favoured by Calvin, who held to the theology of the ascension and was always apprehensive about our innate liking for a 'gross presence' of Christ, and the other by Luther, who held to the realism of the incarnation and always distrusted too ethereal a spiritualization of Christ's presence. As we know, it was there that the tragic break between reformers took place, in connection with the Lord's Supper.

[11] We recall that J. Héring thought that the expressions in Colossians preceded those in Rom. 6, for instance, and that Paul was supposed to go into reverse gear, as it were, so as to avoid the ethical and spiritual confusion caused by a too venturesome assertion of 'our resurrection with Christ' (cf. *En Christ*, pp. 51ff.).

There is no need to continue the quotation; everyone knows the text of Col. 3.1–4, as well as Ephesians 1 and 2, where the author goes further: being raised up, we are made to 'sit with him in the heavenly places in Christ Jesus'. There is nothing speculative about these bold declarations; we have seen that they correspond to a pastoral concern and follow from the line of argument belonging to these epistles. Time gives way to place, and now that Christ has been raised the drama of salvation has moved into the heavenly spheres. To that place, therefore, the Christians of Ephesus and Colossae had to have the triumphal assurance of their redemption transferred; they had to be prevented from allowing themselves to be drawn away, as they previously had been, by 'the elemental spirits of the universe', or to lapse into slothfulness; when the Church went into action it had to pitch its camp in face of the aeons and the principalities at the critical point of the opposition; it had to develop the idea of Christ as the sovereign 'head' of the universe as well as of his own Body; in fact, the heavenly places 'with him', in God, had to be made the centre of gravity of our existence. He is not alone in glory—'he led a host of captives' (Eph. 4.8). Round about him the community of the elect, even of those who are still living on earth, both Jews and Greeks, allows God to set against the heavenly powers the living demonstration of the unsearchable wisdom of the plan realized in Christ.

Thus the Church is called, first of all, to live in such close communication with the 'Head' that it can demonstrate the reconciliation of Israel and the Gentiles in complete unity (whence the injunctions to the Church to 'grow up in every way into him who is the head', and the views on the building up of the Body and the ministries); but it is also called to take part by praise and prayer (which here take on a special importance) in a fight which, going beyond flesh and blood, is directed against thrones and lordships—i.e. the forces that transcend mankind. And after all, what we personally have to do is to 'seek the things that are above'—such solid realities as mercy, humility, meekness, patience, peace, love, forgiveness, praise (cf. Col. 3). These 'good things to come' are, in fact, henceforth inseparable from him 'in whom are hid all the treasures of wisdom and knowledge' (Col. 2.3).

In these letters, therefore, the personal relation to the 'Head' never assumes an exclusively mystical tone that breaks away from churchly considerations (the need for building up the Body) or from ethical exhortations (the movement of community life, described in Col. 3 as the incessant course of God's grace which, after irrigating the lives of the elect, returns to him in thanksgivings). But this union, which is of itself enough to reveal the specifically Christian inspiration of letters that are often suspected of harbouring gnostic elements, must not be allowed to obscure the light that the texts throw on the nature of personal relationship with Christ.

We must put aside at once any idea of a continual state of rapture that would enable the Christian to join his glorified Lord now and for ever. That would be very unlike what we know of Paul, and in any case it would contradict the experience that he brings forward in self-defence in II Cor. 12: what would there be extraordinary about being mysteriously caught up to the third heaven if that were to be the Christian's permanent condition? Could we speak of the *hidden* life if it were unveiled to us before the appointed time, i.e. before the parousia of the Lord who will be its supreme revelation?

So 'with Christ', the focal point where the various threads of our past and future existence meet, is kept from us for the moment. Life in Christ is out of our reach, beyond our experience; we can only believe in it and live it in submission to the Lord who is its sole depositary. It is a question of our own life, which we do not control, although we have the entire responsibility for it. It remains as if guarded from our disqualifications and kept in a safe place for the day of its unveiling. It is like the gold bars that lie in the vaults of a bank and cover the value of the paper money that passes from hand to hand and deteriorates a little every time it is used. Its value is not in the paper, or in the design, or in the watermark, but in the one signature that certifies that it is worth its value in gold. Baptism certifies in like manner that our aimless, futile life takes its value from that of Jesus, who is its reality hidden in God.[12] What we can see of it is never the criterion; the only thing that counts is the promise that has been ratified concerning it. Thus the Lord is allowed absolute freedom to manifest

---

[12] J. Baruzi speaks of a kind of 'transcreation of our self', *Création religieuse* I, p. 79.

himself when he wishes. The Christian has nothing to fear. He acknowledges that Christ has the right to come or to tarry; salvation never depends on these visitations. If Jesus reveals himself, he greets him with humility and joy. If Jesus hides his face, he is not forsaken. Even if he is caught up to the third heaven where all is revealed, it is not the words that are heard there that will edify the Church, but those that are received in weakness and struggle: 'My grace is sufficient for you.'

(b) The presence of Christ

The Lord, who is close to God, is also among us and in us; life in Christ is made real by the miracle of his presence. But let us not be ensnared by words. The concept of 'presence' is not the apostle's, and the undeniable reality of Christ's presence does not stem from a special category; it is dynamic, an effective power that remains relative to its own context, to God's glory and the Church's mission. It tells us that we are entering the final stage of the story of salvation, the last days, when Israel's Lord fulfils in Jesus Christ the prophetic promise to set up his dwelling among his people. But even there the apostle avoids speaking of Christ's *dwelling-place* in us. Eph. 3.17 is an exception, and confirms once more the special style of that letter. In contrast, Paul speaks several times of the *Spirit* that 'dwells in you' (Rom. 8.9, 11; I Cor. 3.16). That expression, though it conveys the idea of the gift of the *pneuma*, may in fact, mislead us as to our relationship with the Lord. Perhaps we have the reason in I Cor. 6, where Paul writes 'Do you not know that your bodies are members of Christ?' (v. 15) and then 'Do you not know that your body is a temple of the Holy Spirit within you?' (v. 19). As Christ has become, in his body, God's real dwelling-place, he cannot at the same time be the one who lives in it; and, by similar reasoning, it will not do to say that he inhabits our bodies; taken singly they will never be his body, but his own members, and together they form, in him, the house consecrated to God, the dwelling-place of the Spirit.[13]

Nor must we forget what exegesis tells us: the expression 'Christ in us' is rare by comparison with *in Christo*; they do not

---

[13] We can feel the slight differences that distinguish the Johannine expression from a mysticism that is nevertheless close to it in its inspiration.

Communion with Christ

form the neat pair so dear to the theologians, and the former does not appear in what might be called the apostle's mystical texts.[14] We may remember that, speaking generally, it emerges as the incontestable fact to which the apostle appeals in order to intimate clearly to his correspondents that they have irrevocably begun the last stage.

But the very force of this appeal, the fact that Paul makes it at the crucial moments of his dialectic about faith and law and about making 'the word of God fully known' by the Gentiles' sharing in Christ's body, and also at the crucial moments of his own inward reasonings, and the unforgettable words in which he expresses the intensity of his own experience, have given to certain passages a vitality that has survived the centuries, so that today they still remain for us the amazing revelation of the indisputable presence of the Lord Jesus living in his apostle. . . . 'It is no longer I who live, but Christ who lives in me', 'For me to live is Christ', 'The love of Christ controls us.'[15]

Thus the life of Christ does not simply remain hidden; it must break out and emerge like the spurting of a geyser, and our calling is to be the privileged place where that happens.

If we try to trace it, we think at once of the Lord's Supper. We shall refer to this in chapter III; and meantime it does not seem in Paul's writings to play the part of unveiling an invisible presence. Nor can we start from the exceptional texts of the apostle's conversion. He regarded the appearance of the risen Lord as a *revelation* of Jesus Christ (Gal. 1.12, 15). But he always related the meeting on the Damascus road to the irrevocable events that are at the root of the Christian tradition (I Cor. 15.1–9), and not to the permanent condition of Christ's servant. The most significant texts are in II Corinthians. We know that the critics, in view of the diversity of accent and the sudden changes of cadence, generally think it is a composite document made up of different pieces fitted together. But even so, it seems to us to show an underlying unity that gravitates round the ministry of the new covenant (called the

[14] The main passages are Gal. 2.20; Col. 1.27; Gal. 4.19; Eph. 3.17; II Cor. 13.5; Rom. 8. In all the texts the expression is in the plural, and can just as well mean 'among' as 'in' us (you). There is one exception, the singular of Gal. 2.20, which gives the verse still more force. See *En Christ*, pp. 80ff.

[15] This last verb is difficult to translate; it suggests both the idea of enclosing or gripping, as when someone is held between two hands, and a movement that some have rendered by 'pressing' or 'squeezing'.

diakonia of the Spirit, of justification, of the gospel, and of reconciliation). The sharp dispute concerns the credentials of the ambassador Paul of Tarsus, and in the defence of their authenticity there emerges more and more clearly the idea of revelation.

When he was at grips with the worst difficulties, from within as well as from without, Paul could have taken refuge in 'the life hidden with Christ in God'; on the contrary, he nowhere allows the Lord's presence to be more forcefully revealed: this is the moment of discovery.[16] That presence is inscribed upon the community at Corinth, a letter that is destined to be read and reread, and which conveys the glory of God working in Christ; it is felt in the person of the minister of the gospel, who is himself redolent of Christ; it is shown in the apostle's bodily sufferings, his flesh becoming the epiphany of the life of Christ; it shines on the faces of those who reflect the glory of Christ's face and are changed in to his likeness from glory to glory.

And we must not make these texts say that this Christ is the Spirit; we have made short work of the wrong interpretations of II Cor. 3.17, which, by confusing the *Kyrios* and the *pneuma*, keep us from a deeper understanding of the apostle's mysticism; is it not striking that there appears at the heart of this section, in the decisive passage (4.5), the most human name that he can give to his Lord, and the name which he completely identifies with the one who lived on earth—that of *Jesus*?

But if this presence really is Jesus, it is he whom we no longer know 'from a human point of view' (II Cor. 5.16). We now have no immediate access to him. He makes himself known in his very absence: he reveals himself to us through what he has been and what he will be.[17] The communion of love cannot yet dispense with faith or hope. Personal relationship will therefore need some mediation; if we were not afraid to introduce a dogmatic vocabulary here, we should say that that mediation appeals to a double witness—the outward witness of the apostles, and the inward witness of the Spirit.

---

[16] We see the development of successive themes: in Christ the veil is taken away; it is taken away from the Scripture, from God's face, from the believers' faces; in that glorious light, consciences and faces are brought into the sight of the Lord and of men. It is the witness with no disguise who pleads Paul's case and confounds his opponents, the 'superlative apostles', who put a smoke-screen round their designs and their associates, and can thus distort the gospel of God.

[17] Cf. *En Christ*, conclusions of ch. IV.

Communion with Christ

(i) *Christ's presence is bound up with the apostles' witness*

What, in fact, distinguishes the Lord's presence from all other mystical experience is that it is that of Israel's Messiah, Christ Jesus. Those who had been able to meet Jesus and know him never had the slightest doubt of the risen Lord's identity with the crucified one. It was a recognition to which the story of Emmaus testifies in an unforgettable way. For Paul it was the object of a special dispensation bound up with his apostolic calling: the 'revelation' of Christ in him, with no human intermediary, was felt to be an exceptional event, just because of its direct nature—so exceptional that, as we have seen, the apostle connected this appearance with the events of the normative revelation of Christ. The risen Lord presented himself to him as 'Jesus of Nazareth', and Saul's ministry, the goad against which it would have been hard for him to kick, was at once to become for others the intermediary that allowed them, not only to discover in Jesus the Christ whom the prophets had promised, but also conversely to find in Paul's Lord, in the giver of the Spirit and the master of the community, the Jesus who had been crucified some time before. There is no escape from this testimony, for apart from it the history of Jesus, equally with the Lord's presence in us, would be incomprehensible—on the one hand a life that is over, which, if we are aware of it, we can now only admire, and on the other hand a presence hardly distinguishable from the various psychic or suggestive phenomena and impossible to sift out of the arcana of mystical experience in general, like a photograph of which we possess only the negative, the positive being beyond our reach, in the apostle's testimony. That testimony reaches us today, not only through the living chain of 'imitators of Christ', the bearers of his word, but also through the Scripture—like the two sets of lenses in a pair of field-glasses, which put the view in focus; the eye-pieces have to be adjusted in relation to each other, but the Scriptures are always needed for reference; they are the irreplaceable indicator which, being illuminated by the Spirit, alone enables us to identify him who lives *in us* with him who has lived *for us*. They give Christ's presence its holiness[18] at the same time that

---

[18] I.e. its divine otherness.

they take us into its depths; they preserve the irreducible nature of the person whom they reveal.[19]

But does not this take us quite beyond Paul's horizon, which nowhere admitted any written and canonized form of apostolic witness? We have seen how useless it was to look for any foreshadowing of this in his letters, by patiently collecting occasional signs, recollections, phrases, allusions bearing on the 'life of Jesus'.[20] What points much more to the need of external confirmation is the bond of unity that Paul maintained, in spite of all the opposition, delays, and obstacles his work encountered, with the other apostles, the Jerusalem church, and the Lord's brother James—in short, with all those who had been Jesus' companions. Further evidence of this need is that other bond of unity that Paul did not hesitate to establish between his own experience and the Old Testament writings. This, more than the harmonizing efforts of conservative exegesis, is significant of the vital part played by the witnesses of Jesus' past. Is it not remarkable that today the most alert of Bultmann's disciples feel it necessary to return to the historical person of the one whom only the Synoptic Gospels allow us to know otherwise than as the *pneuma*?

(ii) *Christ's presence is bound up with the gift of the pneuma*

We need only note a few characteristics of the analogies and differences in a relationship that can now be regarded as established.[21] In the first place Christ's presence is eschatological in the sense that it is characteristic of the covenant of the last days. Foreshadowed by the deliverance recorded in Exodus, consecrated by the system of worship and the regulations laid down as to holiness, proclaimed by the prophets as the glorious messianic reality, the coming of the Lord among his own, the dwelling of God amid his people, is made real by Christ's life in us. We need only recall Romans 8, or quote Gal. 2.20: 'It is no longer I who live, but Christ who lives in me.' The apostle's personal experience is brought home to the Galatians for the same reason as is the gift

---

[19] Cf. J. Baruzi, *op. cit.*: 'Thus there is a mysticism of Christ, but it is based on a recollection beyond the mystics' reach': our memory here is the Synoptic Gospels. Out of their context, Paul's epistles themselves would produce only a phantom of Christ!

[20] Cf. *En Christ*, p. 99; the personal characteristics that one picks out are all kerygmatic, and not biographical.

[21] Cf. *En Christ*, pp. 61ff., and also T. Preiss's exposition, *Le témoignage intérieur du Saint-Esprit* (CT 13), 1946.

of the Spirit that they have received (Gal. 3.2)—to make plain to them that the régime of the law has been replaced by that of faith, that of 'the promise'. It means, secondly, that that presence is spiritual: it no longer depends on physical recognition (II Cor. 5.16); even if it motivates all our being and can create emotional reactions, psychic or mystical, it belongs to the spiritual world to come, which Christ finally entered from the time of his resurrection. Like the gift of the *pneuma*, it is for the believer the guarantee of the Kingdom and of his own final transfiguration; it thus relates to our inmost selves, to that inner being that represents the germ of the new creation. Thirdly, it is present, placed like the gift of the Spirit, and by him, into God's today which creates our present time by allowing us to share here and now in his salvation and in all its history. It is no use our trying to go back into the past to become Jesus' contemporaries, to seek him in the times that are gone so as to make him either survive or come to life again; and it is no use our trying to go forward into the future and anticipate the time of the parousia; we have not to ascend, descend, or suspend the course of time, for the meeting is the great reality of existence that allows us today to commune with him who is, and was, and is to come. Finally, Christ's presence is personal; any tampering with biblical times simply results in a misrepresentation of Christ's person, as in a distorting mirror; when his identity is called in question there is always the risk that our relationship with him will degenerate into a continued incarnation, or into spiritualization and illuminism. The *pneuma*'s role consists in removing any confusion between him and us, whether its form is substantialist or 'mystical'. It reveals to us the Lord in Christ—therefore someone other than ourselves—and safeguards his holiness, as do the Scriptures, at the same time giving to that intimate experience its own particular character. It confirms both difference and communion in the relationship of two persons, one of whom always remains supreme.[22]

[22] The *pneuma* is the witness and guarantor of the irrevocable nature of the process of salvation. The failure to remember his role has caused three persistent errors in the course of the centuries:

First, Jesus is supposed to be present through a kind of reincarnation, or of continued incarnation (so E. Mersch, *Le corps mystique du Christ*, vol. I, p. 253): 'As Christ, his mystical body is at the same time human and divine, a prolonging of the incarnation, or rather the incarnation itself, but the incarnation in so far as it finishes its own course . . .').

Christianity According to Paul

Two other aspects, relating not now to the nature, but to the purpose of Christ's presence, are still to be mentioned; they characterize his mediating office in relation to the Father and to the world.

(iii) *Christ's presence is election*

Christ's lordship is as total as was his obedience. The miracle of that lordship now allows him, in his sovereign freedom, to take and claim the apostle's life for himself; he has redeemed it and acquired it. He is free to *choose* this or that life, so that it may become in this world a place and manifestation of his will, his grace, and his resurrection. Thus Paul's life and temperament, his style and letters (so Pauline) appear in their full and free individuality, in their characteristic strength and weaknesses, as a revelation of the very life of Christ in this world. Through him Christ follows out his ministry, he speaks, he acts—in a word, he is there. In his mysterious choice, God takes the risk of handing over to that life the task of witnessing to his own Son's coming among men. Even if Jesus' presence floods the heart with joy and love, at the same time as leading to difficult struggles and 'much affliction', it is always bound up with the redemptive plan, the preaching of the gospel to the ends of the earth. To give an example, we have seen that the exclamation 'It is no longer I who live, but Christ who lives in me' was meant to be taken in its context, not as a mystical bestowal, but as a sign given to the Galatians of their new condition before God; it gives rise to the entreaty 'Brethren, I beseech you, become as I am, for I also have become as you are' (4.12), and to the struggle that is involved in the ministry: 'My little children, with whom I am again in travail until Christ be formed in you!' (4.19).

Jesus is supposed to be present, secondly, through faith that takes us back and makes us contemporary with the apostle and with Christ (so Kierkegaard); or, thirdly, by the Christian's attempt to actualize the past, so as to 'make Christ live again' (so certain pietistic or liberal lines of thought in the nineteenth century).

When the 'once for all' of the time of the incarnation is obliterated, because the part of the *pneuma* has been misconceived, the damage finally inflicted is on the identity of Jesus' person. This remains unchanged in so far as we keep to the decisive character of his passage on earth, as that is where he made himself known, once for all. Thus the Spirit, as guarantor of the 'once for all', also guarantees the identity of Christ's person and maintains its otherness; thanks to him all diffusion of Christ in the world, all confusion between the Church and its Lord, and all fusion of Jesus and the believer, are avoided. As soon as the Spirit's part is forgotten, these errors appear again in the history of the Church or of religious devotion.

Communion with Christ

Christ's presence in Paul, then, is not an end in itself—it is not so much his presence in Paul as his presence in the world through Paul; far from capturing attention and monopolizing the stage, it is increasingly humble, so as to become dead to itself and a resurrection for others—in a word, a *calling*. It is neither the crowning of a slow ascent nor the conquest of an intense religious life; from the outset it is shown as grace along the ways of the gospel. The Lord within us leads us unwearyingly to the Lord outside us, waiting for us in humblest of our brothers, in the tasks, the pleasures, and the troubles 'in his name'. The extraordinary treasure that fills the 'earthen vessel' is shown to be, not some indescribable bestowal, but Christ's glorious gospel whose minister Paul has become; and is it not much more in his vision of men and things than in all his confidences that we can finally grasp the wonderful reality of his Saviour's presence in him? Does not the passage, already quoted, from Eph. 3.17, show us that the result of Christ's dwelling in our hearts is to open them to the boundless horizons of God's love?

It is therefore no surprise that the apostle has not had to resort to any special vocabulary to express the communion that unites him with Christ. In particular the language of the love-relationship, so beloved of mystics both before and after him, is foreign to him. The Lord's only bride is the Church (Eph. 5.22ff.); the only betrothed whom he has led to Christ is the community in Corinth —not his own soul (II Cor. 11.2). Love's communion is not the kind of bond that might be formed between two people who incline toward each other; Paul is gripped by a love that dwells in him and dominates his whole being: the love that Christ in him bears to the Philippians (Phil. 1.8) and to all men (II Cor. 5.14).

Thus the most personal relationship will use the simplest and baldest language, not language that describes exceptional states, but that which is used about ordinary things. It is made quite plain in the relationship between master and servant, king and ambassador, lord and envoy. This may seem rather commonplace, but if we have grasped anything of the realism of the Bible, we discover there, on the contrary, the most complete expressions of the epiphany of Jesus of Nazareth in Paul of Tarsus. He has set him apart, made him his own, sent him—so much so that the apostle can write without self-glorification, 'You . . . received me . . . as Christ Jesus' (Gal. 4.14). In the most complete humility, is it possible to be more totally identified with the Lord of glory?

(iv) *Christ's presence and divine sonship*

Christ's presence is not an end in itself; we have seen its aspect as a calling, but we cannot leave it without mentioning its first horizon, which is at the same time its ultimate purpose. It has been possible rightly to insist on the Christocentric nature of Pauline mysticism; but it would be a complete misconception to let it shut itself up, as if Christ were its final aim, as if it would veil the Creator there instead of revealing him. At first sight Paul does not seem as anxious as John to name the Father and to map out untiringly the road that leads from the Father to the Son and from the Son to the Father; but we have recognized the instrumental value of *in Christo*, which is ineffaceable and indicates its mediating function; and we have also seen, more and more clearly, that God is the ground of every action in Christ. The place granted to the Son is not taken away from the Father, any more than the Spirit's action interferes with the Son's; on the contrary, the mighty work of the *pneuma* shows the incessant intervention of the *Kyrios*, and this intervention carries to completion the plans of the God of the covenant.

For anyone who doubts this, a glance at the epistles will provide an abundance of texts. God is the Lord of history from beginning to end; everything comes from him (I Cor. 11.12) and everything exists for him (I Cor. 8.6).[23] He is the Creator (Rom. 4.17) and the provider (II Cor. 9.10); he works in our will and our actions (Phil. 2.13), and no one may answer him back (Rom. 9.20); he leads the world by his wisdom, according to the mystery of his choice (I Cor. 1–4). He called Abraham, and at the appointed time he fulfilled the promise by sending his Son into the world (Gal. 4.4). His love and righteousness are shown in the vicarious sacrifice of Jesus his servant (Rom. 5.8; 3.21). He gives us universal reconciliation (II Cor. 5.18); it is he who raised Jesus from the dead (Gal. 1.1), raised him above every name (Phil. 2.9), bestowed

---

[23] We have given only one reference on each point. The purpose of this long and perhaps tedious enumeration is to emphasize to the reader that, far from taking anything away from God, Paul ascribes everything to him; there is no Christology that does not end in theology!

his Spirit on us (I Cor. 2.12). The Church is his (I Thess. 2.14); he sustains it by his faithfulness (I Cor. 1.9), builds it up (I Cor. 3.10), gives it the ministers who are needed for its mission (Eph. 4.11); he guides the apostles' steps (I Thess. 3.11), saves by the preaching of the gospel (I Cor. 1.21), and gives eternal life (Rom. 6.23). He is the supreme Judge (Rom. 3.6); he will command the trumpet to sound for the parousia and final resurrection (I Thess. 4.16). Everyone will appear before him (Rom. 14.10–12), and he will reign, world without end (I Cor. 15.28)—his love has overcome everything (Rom. 8.39). So to our God and Father be glory for ever and ever (Phil. 4.20): every tongue shall praise him (Rom. 14.11). Our destiny is to share in that glory, and the world is condemned for having rejected him (Rom. 1.21). As we have been created anew in the Father's likeness, we can repeatedly bless him (II Cor. 1.3), thank him (Rom. 1.8), glorify him in all our being (I Cor. 6.20) with heart and voice (Rom. 15.6), by offering ourselves to him as a living and holy sacrifice (Rom. 12.1), as did Christ himself. Freed from the law, and from sin and death, we belong entirely to him: to live in Jesus Christ is to *live for God* (Rom. 6.11): that is our new and blessed destiny.

But more than this: Paul does not for a moment give the impression that he was conscious of *changing* his God on the day of his conversion: he did not cease to recognize the only God, the God of his fathers, of Abraham, Isaac, and Jacob. A transformation of God would annihilate his whole gospel: is it not the amazing miracle that the God of Israel sent his Son, 'born of woman, born under the law', to obtain our adoption as sons? God's righteousness accomplished his aim—which the law found impossible—by making his Son share in flesh and blood like our own. Baptism in the name of Jesus seals an adoption by pure grace, giving us a share in the Holy Spirit.[24] Henceforth we have access to the inaccessible holiness of the Eternal, and, impelled by the

[24] In Gal. 4.5f., redemption has given us adoption as sons, and the latter has given us the *pneuma*. Rom. 8.14 says that the gift of the Spirit makes us sons of God. This is only an apparent contradiction. As we have seen, the gift of the Spirit is really subordinated to the coming of salvation, and therefore to the declaration of our adoption. But it really effects this adoption from within, putting in us the feelings that were in Jesus Christ, and transforming us into the Son's image to make us children who are like the Father.

Recent studies have re-emphasized baptism as an act of adoption and a source of the gift of the Spirit. Cf. M. A. Chevallier, *L'Esprit et le Messie dans le bas-judaïsme et le christianisme primitif*, Paris, 1958.

Spirit, we are free, with Jesus, to turn to the Lord with the ineffable name and cry 'Abba, Father!'

Thus Christ's presence takes us into the new dwelling-place, 'the household of God', where we have a place as sons; such is the gospel proclaimed to the Galatians. Communion with the First-born fashions them into the image of the Father (Rom. 8.29), teaches them a filial attitude, begins to replace pride by humility, prompts them to that obedience and gratitude that characterize legitimate children; they learn continually from the 'Spirit of the Son' which is shed abroad in their hearts[25] and brings them into the divine depths that only he can plumb, so as to reveal to them 'the gifts bestowed on us by God' (I Cor. 2.11f.).

Being united to the Son, the apostle will realize his destiny as a man and a member of the people of Israel—namely to glorify God till he becomes a means of grace to others, too. It does not surprise us, therefore, to see the epistles carried along in the movement of eucharistic prayer by the burst of uninterrupted praise that rises to the Father of our Lord Jesus Christ. Life *in Christo* has opened people's hearts to the greatness of his love, and the Son has now come to be the head of a new world that is reunited in rediscovered worship; the whole creation sighs as it awaits the revelation of the children of God, so that it, too, may share in their glorious liberty.

4. THE IMITATION OF CHRIST

We have more than once found it advisable to put aside the idea of the imitation of Christ as unsuitable for showing the relationship that unites us with him. Before going farther, let us reread— perhaps we are inclined to do this more on account of spiritual tradition than for the sake of exegesis—the Pauline texts calling us to imitation. They do exist, and it is only fair that if we take exception to them, we should try to find their positive meaning. We may expect some surprises, and this apparent *détour* may claim to put us on a fairly direct route to the churchly reality of communion in Christ.

The texts in which the apostle speaks explicitly of imitation are comparatively few. The principal ones are I Thess. 1.6; 2.14; II

---

[25] This idea lights up the whole of Rom. 8.

Thess. 3.7–9; Phil. 3.17; I Cor. 4.16; 11.1; Eph. 5.1; and to these we may add passages such as Phil. 4.9 and Gal. 4.12.[26]

One thing is obvious at first sight: we are in quite a different climate from that of the *imatatio Christi* as understood by Western piety. In nearly all the texts the apostle puts himself forward, with authority and affection, for his readers to imitate, sometimes naming Christ as well.[27] Once it is the churches of Judea (I Thess. 2.14) that are held up as examples, and once God the Father (Eph. 5.1).[28]

W. Michaelis gives three shades of meaning to the Pauline use of the verb 'to imitate':[29] (1) a comparison (as in I Thess. 2.14); (2) an exhortation to follow the apostle's example—that is, to recognize his authority (II Thess. 3.7–9; Phil. 3.17); and (3) an encouragement to obedience (I Cor. 4.16, where the idea of example is blurred; but also I Cor. 11.1; I Thess. 1.6; Eph. 5.1). Michaelis thus represents the furthest point of what might be called a Protestant interpretation of 'imitation'. In reacting against certain deviations that depreciate the *sola gratia*, we finally empty this idea of all substance by reducing it to a matter of mere exhortation;[30] and that hardly seems to us to conform to the meaning of the texts.

[26] The expression κατὰ κύριον or κατὰ Χριστόν has been interpreted in several ways. Deissmann connects it closely with *in Christo* ('substantially akin'—*Die neutestamentliche Formel* . . ., p. 116 n. 6), whereas C. Bricka contrasts them: 'They are by no means synonymous.' 'To live in Christ' is the soul's mystical union 'with him who dwells at the right hand of the Father. To live according to Christ is the ethical direction of the mind back towards him who was obedient unto death' (*Le fondement christologique* . . ., pp. 50f.). He therefore understands it in the sense of the imitation or the example of Jesus. Thus he expresses II Cor. 11.17: 'Contrary to the example of humility that Jesus left us', and Rom. 15.5: 'Be conciliatory, as Jesus was.' We need hardly say that we are far from agreeing with this explanation. For Michaelis, κατὰ Χριστόν appeals, not to Christ's example, but to his will (*TWNT* IV, p. 671). These two currents meet again in our biblical versions; the RSV translates Rom. 15.5 'in accord with Christ Jesus' (cf. the Version Synodale: 'as Christ wishes'); the NEB has 'after the manner of Christ Jesus' (cf. the Jerusalem Bible). The preposition probably introduces, as in κατὰ σάρκα or κατὰ πνεῦμα, the idea of a way of life, of the element that determines it. κατὰ κύριον relates to the life of the Church, the will of its leader, and the obedience of its members: 'That is how it is in the Body of Christ.'

[27] I Thess. 1.6; I Cor. 11.1.
[28] This is another detail peculiar to this epistle.
[29] *TWNT* IV, pp. 661ff.
[30] Cf. the justified comments of W. G. Kümmel, HNT 9, pp. 173 and 183, or of C. Masson, CNT XI, p. 21 n. 2: 'Michaelis lays too much stress on the obedience due to the apostle and Christ, and not enough on the example to be followed and the normative character of the behaviour of Christ and the apostle, which, just because it is *according to the Spirit*, excludes all formal imitation produced by diligent effort.'

I Thess. 2.14, then, mentions the churches: 'For you, brethren, became imitators of the churches of God in Christ Jesus which are in Judea, for you suffered the same things. . . .' The resemblance here is obviously not the result of any initiative on the part of the Macedonian churches, wanting to equal those of Palestine; we are still a long way from an Ignatius thirsting for the martyrdom which alone, he feels, will enable him completely to imitate his Lord. The young churches are at grips with the same trials and have undergone the same experiences as their Judean sisters; persecution has stamped on them the sign of their mutual resemblance.

'You became imitators of us and of the Lord; for you received the word in much affliction, with joy inspired by the Holy Spirit; so that you became an example to all the believers in Macedonia and Achaia.' I Thess. 1.6 is particularly significant. The context relates this passage to the beginning of I Corinthians: the apostle calls to mind the circumstances of his preaching, God's power manifested in his person ('You know what kind of men we proved to be among you for your sake'). The message is inseparable from the messenger; his life, his attitudes, his behaviour were there as visible pledges of the Word that he offered to the Thessalonians. So their imitation will not consist merely in similarity of obedience, but their obedience itself will be stimulated and marked by the apostle's personal characteristics which will never again be separated from the gospel that has been received; and it will also be marked by all the affection that they feel for him. But Paul thinks again: it would not do for their final thought to be of himself as such, and so he adds the corrective 'and of the Lord'. By thus recalling the cross, which is the origin of all preaching and is at the heart of all suffering, he emphasizes that he does not impose his authority and example as a man, but as the Lord's appointed servant. And he does not stop there: the Thessalonians in their turn have become models for the churches in Macedonia, just as they themselves have taken as their model the communities of Judea. We begin to see the characteristic feature of imitation in the epistles, namely the live way in which the gospel is propagated, not simply as doctrine or instruction, but as the Word made flesh; at every stage of the journey forward its means of further progress are its past achievements. If we now look at the content of the imitation that we have in mind here (receiving the Word in the midst of tribulation), we find as the echo of the evangelical message, 'If any man would come after me, let him deny himself. . . .' To follow Jesus, the disciples were to be prepared to face persecution, public trial, and the cross; here, to receive the Word, they enrol in a similar line of succession, before they in turn become a link in that tradition. We are watching a transposition of the primitive *Nachfolge*, which we might term, speaking etymologically, the sequence—or, if we think of the community, the consequence, the following together—of Christ.

We find in II Thess. 3.7–9 the same thought of a tradition whose authority is derived from the two poles of the Word and its bearer. This time we are bordering on ethics; the question of work follows that of the reception of the Word. Paul does not present himself here as a model to imitate, but as an example to follow. He has abstained from apostolic privileges, working day and night with his hands so as to live up to his teaching, offering freely what he had freely received, while taking care not to give, in his conduct, any pretext for a wrong interpretation of the freedom brought by the gospel, or any opening for illuminism or apocalyptic divagations.

Phil. 3.17–18 denounces the intrigues of the false brethren who are prowling round the Philippians, and round Paul himself, all through this joyful epistle.[31] In the confusion of a conflict in which the new converts do not always know to whom to turn, Paul stands here as a landmark at the cross-roads. He is a rallying-point on the way to the cross—he who, like his Master, has renounced every other prerogative. Yet he does not for a moment isolate himself as a hero on a pedestal: others are there with him, showing in their lives, too, what it means to be a disciple of the crucified one. The stimulation is mutual.

We see the apostle's role again in Phil. 4.9: 'What you have learned and received ($\pi\alpha\rho\epsilon\lambda\acute{\alpha}\beta\epsilon\tau\epsilon$) and heard and seen in me, do.' Teaching, tradition, and personal conduct are again explicitly connected with each other, the various elements being joined together to give full authority to the apostolic word. As Lohmeyer remarks, with a touch of humour, we get our first view here of 'the canonization of Paul in his life and doctrine'.

---

[31] On the identification of the 'enemies of the cross' see Bonnard, CNT X, *ad loc.*

Support is given by two texts in I Corinthians. 'I became your father in Christ Jesus through the gospel. I urge you, then, be imitators of me . . .' (I Cor. 4.15b–17). The brethren at Corinth are not exhorted to become spiritual fathers (even if that is what many of them were!). Nor must we give 'imitation' here an absolute sense that would make it the means of and the road to salvation: 'The bond of spiritual paternity owes everything to the faithful transmission of the gospel, which is its motive force.'[32] And imitation is concerned with one of the critical points of the *Nachfolge*: the Corinthians, being incapable of following the apostle along the road of renunciation, 'have become kings' as if the time for that had already come; they want the crown without the cross. Paul feels impelled to send Timothy to the rescue. The missionary orders to the 'beloved and faithful child in the Lord' correspond exactly to what Paul meant when he said, 'Be imitators of me.' Timothy is enjoined to remind them of the apostle's 'ways in Christ',[33] 'those that he teaches in all the churches'.[34] To imitate the apostle, to keep to the way—it is the same thing. Similarly in the Gospels, *mutatis mutandis*, we have to follow Jesus, to enter the Kingdom. We must not neglect the part played by the figure of the messenger any more than we must underestimate the person of the confessor in Matt. 16,[35] for example, in favour of preaching separated from flesh and blood or of a profession of faith from the person who makes it; that would be in both cases to forget the role of Jesus' person—what would become of the Sermon on the Mount without the one who preached it?

We do not know whether, as J. Héring suggests, the second passage, I Cor. 11.1 ('Be imitators of me, as I am of Christ'), presupposes that Paul knew Christ during his lifetime.[36] Everything leads us to suppose that the apostle is thinking less of Jesus

---

[32] M. Ferrier-Welti, *La transmission de l'Evangile*. This study of the Pastoral Letters contains noteworthy analyses of all these themes.

[33] We must give the word 'way' its proper meaning, which is suggested by the antitheses of I Cor. 4.8–13, and its figurative sense suggested by the verb 'to teach.'

[34] Referring to this passage, J. M. Robinson emphasizes the deep-rooted analogy between 'the existential meaning of Jesus' and the interpretation that the apostle gives us of his own life (vv. 8–13) an interpretation that finally merges in the *kerygma*. That analogy justifies and gives authority to the injunction 'Be imitators of me' (*New Quest* . . ., p. 123).

We have not mentioned I Cor. 4.6 ('. . . That you may learn by us . . .'), in view of the obscurity of the text (cf. Kümmel in HNT 9, *ad loc.*).

[35] Cf. our article 'Pierre et le temps de l'Eglise', *Foi et Vie*, 1954.

[36] CNT VII, *ad loc.*

Communion with Christ

the Galilean than of the *kerygma* that concerns him. 'Christ did not please himself' is a reference not simply to Jesus' altruistic nature but to the supreme sacrifice. Paul has been 'conformed' in his turn, and the Corinthians are urged to allow themselves to be stamped in the same likeness. This is one of the signs of belonging to Christ to which the apostle attaches the greatest importance; he comes back to it many times, and it occasions the lyrical passage of Philippians 2. In the καθὼς καί, too, there is a Johannine flavour that we find again in Eph. 5.1. We might base on it a complete theology of the Fourth Gospel, where it forms the dynamic movement of revelation and of life, that movement that continues unceasingly from the Father to the Son, from the Son to the disciples, and from one disciple to another in the Paraclete, to return once again to the Father.[37]

We hear the same accents in the context of Eph. 5.1, where we are bidden to be 'imitators of God' by forgiving each other. To imitate God is to enter into his likeness, 'as beloved children' are in the image of their Father, through passing into the reign of his forgiveness. The exhortation reminds us that the bond of sonship is necessarily expressed in that kinship of behaviour. To a Father who forgives, a son who forgives—otherwise he denies his adoption. We find ourselves once more at the heart of the Sermon on the Mount.

W. Michaelis has taken exception to Gal. 4.12 because of the reciprocity introduced between Paul and the brethren: 'I beseech you, become as I am, for I also have become as you are.' On the contrary, this reciprocity in imitation would give the text still more interest if the elliptical construction at the end did not make different interpretations possible and prevent our drawing rigid conclusions from it.[38]

[37] 'As the Father has sent me, even so I send you.' 'If you keep my commandments, you will abide in my love, just as I have kept my Father's commandments and abide in his love.' 'As the Father has loved me, so I have loved you; abide in my love.' These parallels are constantly taken up again between the themes of the christological discourses in John 5–7 and those of the ecclesiological discourses in 14–17.

[38] If we interpret in the light of what follows, we may think, with Lagrange, that this is not so much a case of reasoning as of a passionate wish for unity: Paul has taken the first steps; now may the brethren respond on their side! If we put the emphasis on what precedes, we can see an allusion by the apostle, either to his condition before his conversion, or to his renunciations as an evangelist by which he identifies himself with those whom he wishes to gain for Christ (I Cor. 9.20f.). See Bonnard, CNT IX, *ad loc.*

Christianity According to Paul

Albert Schweitzer thinks that our modern sensitivity may be shocked by the way in which Paul offers himself as an example to his readers.[39] These various passages may well be among those where the consciousness of his apostolic authority is shown most clearly. But such is the nature of that apostolate that he seeks not to set himself up, but rather to set himself forth, so that Christ may appear and be served. If, therefore, we are surprised to find that the apostle puts himself forward rather than Christ, as an example to be followed, it does not mean that his own personality is meant to eclipse his Lord's. Only in so far as he has conformed himself to Jesus Christ can he offer himself, not as mediator, but rather as the second link in an unbroken chain, or as the necessary relay station in a television system, so that the picture can be transmitted to the screen. One imitates what is in front of one, and it is the apostle's privilege, as well as his responsibility, to be himself the direct imitator of Christ. We think, with Michaelis, that this upsets current ideas about 'imitation'. But it is not by eliminating Paul's personal role that we rediscover the epistles' original perspective. It is not a matter of arriving, one after the other, at communion with Christ by repeating his deeds and movements. But everything originates in him, in Jesus of Nazareth; he has been appointed the Lord of the Church, and from generation to generation he imprints his character by a living tradition in which, across all the diversity of individuals and communities, his own individuality does not cease to reveal itself as the Word that is always transcendent and always bound up, in its authority and its holiness, with those who are its unworthy bearers.

Finally, we repeat that the invitation to follow the apostle never appears as the condition of justification. Along the way that believers have taken, the apostle comes like a careful trainer, stimulating them, putting them on their feet again, giving them practice when they need it to avoid any breakdown. Renunciation, self-denial, steadfastness in persecution, forgiveness of wrongs, kindness to one's neighbour—these seem to have been, from the Church's earliest times till our own day, the vital things that need to be shown conspicuously and personally if the salvation offered in Christ is to take root in us, those very things in which, in the first place, Jesus had invited his own people to follow him.

[39] *Mysticism*, p. 330.

III

COMMUNION IN CHRIST

THE mystical aspect of *in Christo* has been put in opposition to its ecclesiological sense, or at any rate the attempt has often been made to differentiate them. But personal relationship with the Lord, as it has taken shape little by little, has appeared to us more and more clearly to depend on a reality that gives it its true dimension—God's plan for the world's salvation. In a study that has helped us repeatedly, E. Percy, who is specially concerned to bar the way to any idea of amalgamation, tries to establish the pre-existence of the Body of Christ in relation to those who are its members. Unfortunately this leads him to suggest two successive moments for the believer: first, his entering into Christ, and, secondly, his joining the rest of the faithful. If one may put it so, he distinguishes between a preliminary junction that would connect us to Christ personally, and another link that would join the members together.[1]

It is difficult to believe that there could have been any such dichotomy, either exegetically, or historically, or theologically, or psychologically. The experience of Paul himself was as much in the Church as personal; he discovered in the revelation of the Lord that Jesus was present in the very people whom he was persecuting; his resurrection with Christ was accomplished in Ananias' welcome, the laying on of hands, and baptism. Was there any difference, for those who believed, between adhering to Christ and entering the messianic community? How can one receive the apostles' word without joining in with the apostles? When Acts speaks of those who were 'added to the Lord' (11.24), does it not mean that they joined the Church? Would there be any connection with the Body independently of the members? 'Just as the body is one and has many members . . . so it is with Christ' (I Cor. 12.12). Our meeting with the living Christ is that of

---

[1] *Der Leib Christi*, p. 46.

Christianity According to Paul

'*Christus als Gemeinde existierend*',[2] if one may use Bonhoeffer's forceful expression.

Perhaps, for convenience of exposition, we have here made some sacrifice to a classical, or at least Protestant, tradition, by beginning with personal relationship. This may have some value at a time when, even in the Church, collective life tends to take the place of personal conviction, and community standards are not always high. It would, indeed, have been more in conformity with our analysis of the evolution of the expression *in Christo* to start from its churchly aspect; in this connection the study of the phrase 'in the Lord' has been particularly convincing. But we must remember especially how the essential passages referring to death and to life *with Christ* had revealed an unbreakable connection, whether it concerned union with the Lord or communion with those who belong to him:[3] in the verbs that the apostle used, or coined, σvσταυροῦσθαι, συναποθνῄσκειν, συζῆν, etc., the prefix συν- means at once 'with' and 'together'; it was preferred to its classical synonym μετα- because of this ambivalence, and probably also because of its etymology connecting it with κοινός.[4] We are here at the living source of the *koinōnia*, that communion which is fundamentally a sharing.[5] Thus it is plain that from baptism onwards to be united with Christ is to share with others in his *sōma*, in what has happened to him as well as in what will happen to him, and in his *pneuma*. Such is the grace that is bestowed on us and continually renewed, since it is Christ who is continually imparting himself anew[6] by giving us a share in his blood (i.e. his life) and in his Body (i.e. all those whom he unites by distributing to them the same bread). It is significant that through Rom. 6 and I Cor. 10 we at once meet the two constitutive sacraments of *in Christo*. And we know that in the course of the epistles communion with Christ is embodied in actual participation in the gospel (Phil. 1.4) as in the *diakonia* (II Cor. 8.6), in sufferings as in comfort (II Cor. 1.7), in mutual needs as in possessions (Rom. 12.13).

[2] Literally 'Christ existing in the form of the community'.
[3] Cf. *En Christ*, pp. 38ff.
[4] κοινός meant 'common' = 'shared by all', and hence 'profane' (in contrast to 'sacred'—nowadays we would say 'lay' or 'secular') and 'vulgar'. In Rom. 14.14 the AV and RSV have 'unclean' and the NEB 'impure'.
[5] Cf. *TWNT* III, pp. 789ff.
[6] H. von Soden calls the *koinōnia* 'the Lord's self-communication' (*Sakrament und Ethik*, p. 30).

Communion in Christ

Our wish, therefore, is to see in the following pages how union with Christ is lived in brotherly communion, how relationship with the Lord takes shape in the new relationships that are given us in him, thus attempting what might be called a phenomenological approach to the Body of Christ: might there not be here an opening to escape from dilemmas that often lead nowhere, and to clear a way for ourselves between the temptations of idealism and those of an equivocal naturism, between pure symbolism and 'continued incarnation'? Is not the gospel, as has been said, a secret of relationships? Without claiming to make an exhaustive study by ways that are not the most obvious, we should like to get a picture from life of the mysterious network of exchanges and communications through which Christian life is achieved. We could have taken a way that is both recognized and fruitful, and considered, for example, the bringing of social or conjugal relationships under the Lord's rule; but either of these themes would need a treatise to itself.[7] Our more modest aim is to glance at some of the realities of salvation so as to see the working of these new relationships in it: future possessions that are already offered are not private virtues that the individual ought to appropriate; it is only thanks to others that he receives and enjoys them.

We shall now merely appeal to a long exegetical tradition. Here are three quotations from authors as different as possible:

'And if we wish to be held by the body of Christ, let no one be anything for himself, but all that we are, let us be that for others. That is done for charity, and where charity does not reign, there is no edification of the Church, but pure dissipation . . .' (John Calvin).[8]

'Although in the expression of the Pauline mysticism the phrase *in Christo* is linguistically dominant, nevertheless the original conception is constantly breaking through, namely, the sharing by the Elect in the same corporeity with Christ. . . . The union between the Elect and Christ has thus a meaning not only in relation to the Elect, but also in relation to Christ Himself' (Albert Schweitzer).[9]

---

[7] On the social relationship we may refer to the admirable study of T. Preiss 'Life in Christ and Social Ethics in the Epistle to Philemon', in *Life in Christ*, pp. 32ff., where he brings us to the heart of life in Christ. On the conjugal relationship which is equally revealing, we refer, among numerous studies, to that of J. J. von Allmen, *Maris et femmes d'après saint Paul* (CT 29), 1951; see below, ch. IV.

[8] Commentary on Ephesians 4.16.

[9] *Mysticism*, p. 125.

Christianity According to Paul

'The supreme greatness of St Paul is that he could unite in the deepest intimacy of his being the bond that joined him to the risen Christ with that living unity which could be extended indefinitely and which he regarded as humanity regenerated by Christ' (J. Baruzi).[10]

1. IN YOU AS IN CHRIST

We remember the uncompromising way in which Paul completely repudiated any personal prerogative before God and man. Jesus Christ had become, for all time, his only title to glory and the whole basis of his existence (Phil. 3.3ff.; Gal. 6.14). When the divided Corinthians appeal to Peter, Paul, or Apollos, he rebukes them severely: 'Let no one boast of men' (I Cor. 3.21). To appeal to so-and-so is a retrograde step, as if Paul or Apollos could justify one's existence. . . . But does it not seem as if these titles to glory reappear now and then in the apostle's mouth? Do we not read, further on,' You can be as proud of us as we can be of you, on the day of the Lord Jesus' (II Cor. 1.14), or elsewhere, '. . . so that in me you may have ample cause to glory in Christ Jesus' (Phil. 1.26)? Do we see, after the great baptismal shipwreck, the debris of the old causes of confidence or vainglory floating on the surface? Has not the apostle been caught in the course of his missionary activity by some backwash of pastoral pride?[11] He certainly displays no uneasy conscience about it! No, indeed, he has not changed, but the same decision that excluded all fleshly privileges and staked everything on the Lord *includes Christ's people in Christ*. What unites him with Christ unites him with the Corinthians, and what unites him with the Philippians unites him with Christ. Paul's only 'boasting' *in Christo* is expressed in the fact that henceforth, and equally, the members of Christ have become with him what he has become for the others. Consequently, this mutual 'glorification' does not arise from any mutual complaisance. The ardour of the divided Corinthians attached some of them to Paul, others to Apollos, and others rather to Peter, from entirely unspiritual motives. There is no preference here to limit Paul; they are not chosen, for God has elected them and given them to each other, and everything is sub-

---

[10] *Création religieuse* . . ., p. 91. On 'sharing' cf. L. S. Thornton, *The Common Life in the Body of Christ*, 3rd ed., 1950.
[11] We could also quote Phil. 2.16; I Cor. 15.31; II Cor. 8.24.

Communion in Christ

ordinated to that fact. Paul is not ashamed of his not very glorious companions, for he is not ashamed of the Christ whom they have put on; and he invites them, for their part, not to be ashamed of their apostle who has no imposing presence. The glory that they receive from each other comes not from any success, but from Christ alone, from Christ in them as in him. Reference is made several times to the day of Christ, when everything will be finally weighed in the balance; the light of the judgment will show that not in vain have they renounced their prestige and the more glittering connections of this world so as to agree together to have no other 'boast' than Jesus their common Lord, and his people with him.

Along the same line of thought, the apostle expresses his Christian joy, glory, and hope: Where are they, if not in you? he exclaims, addressing the Thessalonians (I Thess. 2.19f.). But it is above all in the letter to the Philippians that he gives these thoughts free rein. First of all, joy. It dominates their aspect, as it had with the brethren of Thessalonica. To rejoice 'in the Lord' —yes, that is to know that he is 'at hand' (Phil. 4.4f.); but joy, an eschatological gift *par excellence*, is already experienced in brotherly communion; before the last day there will be repeated opportunities for it in Paul's hoped-for coming, his reunion with the Philippians (1.25), in the affection and sympathy that exist between them (2.2), even in his possible martyrdom 'poured as a libation upon the sacrificial offering of your faith' (2.17–18). It is this intimacy that reveals most fully the meaning of 'The Lord is at hand.'

We read further on that, in having mercy on Epaphroditus, God had mercy on Paul (2.27), and, just before, that what affects the brethren also affects the apostle's *psyche* (2.19); all his feelings seem to be moved by reactions and interactions set in motion by other people; thus he is literally transformed, *in Christo*. Dependence on the Lord is extended into this interdependence, which, instead of appearing as the chain that binds the condemned man to his companions in misery, reveals the liberating grace of belonging to the same Master.

Philippians 2 gives us a number of expressions that are significant through being put side by side: τὰ ἑαυτῶν, τὰ περὶ ὑμῶν, τὰ χριστοῦ. The first is what Paul also calls 'the flesh', where, as everyone pursues his own self-interest and seeks to establish his own supremacy, individuals insult and rend each other (cf. Gal. 5.15). In the Spirit, on the other hand, there is harmony between the next two expressions: what concerns Jesus Christ is identical with what concerns *you*. At the beginning of the chapter we can follow an equally remarkable contrast between τὰ ἑαυτῶν (twice in vv. 3f.)— that is to say the selfishness of the flesh—and τὸ αὐτό, αὐτή, which is translated 'the same', but which could be rendered equally well by 'common'; these relate to the Philippians' sharing in love, in the Spirit, and in sympathy (v. 1). And the verb φρονεῖν which occurs three times in this passage, brings out emphatically the equivalence of having 'the same mind', being 'of one mind', and having the mind that is 'in Christ Jesus'.[12] Perhaps we have nowhere a more explicit definition of *in Christo*. To embody it, the Philippians' attitude to each other (ἐν ὑμῖν = among yourselves) must proceed from what is 'also in Christ Jesus', i.e. his abasement, his death and resurrection—in short, the events celebrated in the Christological hymn. It is significant that this text of incalculable range was brought into the letter in connection with injunctions as to the Philippians' attitude to each other; the communion of believers is seen as the unfolding, and, in the etymological sense, the explanation of the hymn across time and space.[13] The refusal of all rivalry and self-assertion is what turns Christ's renunciation into divine equality; the humility that we are not surprised to find at the heart of the exhortation expresses the abasement of him who 'was in the form of God', while the preeminence allowed to others (by virtue not of their own merits but of the grace that has been bestowed on them)[14] corresponds in terms to the exaltation of Christ.[15] Lastly, appreciation of other

[12] It is not easy to translate satisfactorily the three uses, which overlap: τὸ αὐτὸ φρονῆτε, τὸ ἓν φρονοῦντες, τοῦτο φρονεῖτε ἐν ὑμῖν ὃ καὶ ἐν Χριστῷ (vv. 2 and 5). φρονεῖν indicates deep personal feelings that determine behaviour, the characteristics that motivate one's being. Cf. P. Bonnard, CNT X, *ad loc*.
[13] There is an analogous exhortation in Phil. 4.2 *(τὸ αὐτὸ φρονεῖν ἐν κυρίῳ)*. This brings out the linking of the phrases *in Christo* and *in* the Lord. In Phil. 2, Paul has stressed the source whence the Church's life proceeds (what has taken place in Christ); in the second passage he insists on its norm, the Lord.
[14] K. Barth, quoted by P. Bonnard, CNT X, *ad loc*.
[15] The ὑπερέχοντες (Phil. 2.3) is answered by ὑπερύψωσεν (see v. 9).

Communion in Christ

people's qualities, and consideration of their interests, are a faithful reflection of the Lord's sovereignty.[16]

This close correlation appears repeatedly in the apostle's writings: II Cor. 13.11, Rom. 12.16, and Rom. 15.5 repeat τὸ αὐτὸ φρονεῖτε.[17] These last two passages belong to the great development of the last part of Romans, which extends these perspectives by coming back continually to the pronoun ἀλλήλους, one another; its reiteration gives a rhythmic sense of reciprocity in the chapters devoted to the Church. It is interesting to consider carefully the sequence of the text. As we know, the epistle has set out the process of salvation by way of the saving events, baptism, the Christian condition, the gift of the Spirit, and the mystery of election. Here it issues in the reality of the Church, not as if falling back to earth after taking off for a daring flight, but as the aim, here and now, of God's plan. The Church's life contrasts with the present age, and is expressed in intellectual, moral, and spiritual nonconformity (12.2). It is worked out as follows: verse 1, the sacrifice of oneself, the offering of one's body so that it may belong to God; verse 2, renewal of the mind, which, illuminated by the revelation of God's 'mystery' (ch. 9–11), has the task of finding out the right ways; verse 3, renunciation of ὑπερφρονεῖν and behaviour characterized by God's wisdom and inspired by humility, the only acknowledgment of grace. All believers, indeed, form only one Body in Christ, and are members of one another, each having his place (v. 4); charismatic gifts are fitted into the life of the whole (vv. 6ff.), which will be rightly expressed in terms of ἀλλήλους: mutual love, mutual respect, refusal to judge one another, mutual friendliness—everything has to be rewritten.

The 'eccentric' character of the Christian condition is shown more conspicuously: its centre of gravity has shifted from the self to Christ, in the Lord and his members. This, however, does not mean a kind of indefinite horizontal extension—mutual relationships remain at the same time concentric, that means in permanent dependence on the Spirit; they bring us back to the Lord himself,

---

[16] P. Bonnard analyses the difficulties of v. 3, and proposes the translation 'qualities' (CNT X, *ad loc.*).

[17] In Rom. 15.5 we find the expression κατὰ Χριστόν, on which see p. 53 n. 26. We said there that it introduced the idea of a way of life, and of the element that determines it. This means 'as it is in the Body of Christ', invoking at once an external and an internal authority.

Christianity According to Paul

whose sovereignty is exerted every moment, without being diluted in the life of the Body. Heteronomy does not change into autonomy; we are 'under the law of Christ' (I Cor. 9.21). We are given an indication of this in Romans 14, where the apostle, who elsewhere exhorts us to become servants of one another, reminds us forcefully that at the last everyone is responsible for himself before Christ alone. As to opinions expressed on the attitude of one or another, he writes indeed (Rom. 14.4), 'Who are you to pass judgment on the servant of another (i.e. of Christ)? It is before his own master that he stands or falls.' A word comes back here that seemed to be banished from the Church, as it describes what belongs to a person individually;[18] it is written large on what we have so far been able to describe, as if to define the boundary that will always exist between the Christian community and an undifferentiated mass; none of us is interchangeable, the body's members remain persons, and every person is distinguished from the rest through his calling and through his final responsibility before the Lord. But this does not contradict the apostle's conclusion: 'None of us lives to himself, and none of us dies to himself. If we live, we live to the Lord, and if we die, we die to the Lord' (14.7–8).[19]

We still have to go back to the source—to the Lord's Supper and to baptism, which the apostle regards as constitutive elements of the Body of Christ. Each will bring us, in its own way, its decisive confirmation. As to baptism, three passages need to be quoted here: I Cor. 12.13; Gal. 3.26–29; and Col. 3.9–11.

'... So it is with Christ. For by one Spirit we were all baptized into one body—Jews or Greeks, slaves or free—and all were made to drink of one Spirit.'

'For in Christ Jesus you are all sons of God, through faith. For as many of you as were baptized into Christ (εἰς Χριστόν) have put

---

[18] ἴδιος is the opposite of κοινός, but it has not necessarily the egotistical character of the reflexive. Hauck notes that this adjective corresponds to an individual reality unknown to the East and supposed to be a legacy of the Greek genius (*TWNT* III, p. 791). But we must not forget that prophets like Ezekiel, while not putting it in opposition to the community of Israel, could vigorously proclaim the personal responsibility of every individual.

[19] We may again mention the contrast between ἑαυτόν and κύριος.

on Christ. There is neither Jew nor Greek, there is neither slave nor free, there is neither male nor female; for you are all one in Christ Jesus (ἐν Χριστῷ).'

'Do not lie to one another, seeing that you have put off the old nature with its practices and have put on the new nature, which is being renewed in knowledge after the image of its creator. Here there cannot be Greek and Jew, circumcised and uncircumcised, barbarian, Scythian, slave, free man, but Christ is all, and in all.'

Although there are slight differences, these texts have too many similarities for them to be put down merely to recollections; all three depend on part of a baptismal catechism or liturgy that was already highly elaborated—it is of little consequence whether this belonged to the Pauline churches or to the apostle himself. In any case, it is the significance of Christian baptism that is in question, and it is interesting to see how these texts are introduced into the relevant passages, and what they imply.

In I Cor. 12.13, Paul exhorts the Corinthians to acknowledge the unity of the Spirit, the source of varied gifts expressed in different ministries. He appeals to the baptism that they have all received and that has united them into one single Body whose reality transcends the social, racial, or religious categories that had so far differentiated them. If the diversity of conditions, far from impairing the Body's unity, makes it obvious, then in the same way in this Body the diversity of charismatic gifts, far from tearing it to pieces, gives it life and builds it up. Oneness of baptism and unity of the Spirit go together.

Gal. 3.26–29 brings us to another issue: Paul contrasts the régime of the law with that of the promise. Having been for a long time under the tutelage of the law, we have now, through faith, become sons in Christ. The result of baptism has been to put us in him, to *clothe us in Christ*. This image does not evoke, as do the mystery ceremonies, a symbolic individual transformation; it rather transcribes, under a form common to all believers, the change of condition described by Paul in Philippians 3. Having stripped off the other garments and been dispossessed, in baptism, of every prerogative, of every dignity, and of all sense of their own righteousness before the law, the believers have, in common, put on a new garment, Christ, who has become their *raison d'être*, their righteousness before God's judgment-seat itself,[20] so that there is no longer Jew, nor Greek, nor slave. . . .

In I Corinthians the apostle took for granted the diversity of situations that co-existed in the unity of the body, while here in Galatians he seems to abolish them. In reality the reasoning is the same. In I Corinthians we read the middle proposition; in Galatians, as in Colossians further on, the conclusions. The negative phrasing could not sweep out of the Church sex, race, or class, which were still talked about; we need only mention, as quite close to Paul, Gaius and Barnabas, Aquila and Priscilla, Onesimus and Philemon. We do not here enter a domain of general confusion that would obliterate God's creative riches, nor a dull egalitarianism.[21] On the contrary. But for all, without distinction, the major event of existence has stepped in. The baptismal stripping has wrenched from particularist attributes any final and valid title. This has been so acutely felt in the Pauline churches that the apostle can come back to it, both to assert the unity of the Spirit and to make the Galatians conscious of the decisive nature of justification by faith: to 'put on Christ' will henceforth enable everyone to realize his real calling. It is only by living together in one Body that everyone can come to see in his own life the revolutionary reality of baptism. In Christ, and through our fellows, everyone at last becomes himself, the Jew thanks to the Gentile and the Gentile thanks to the Jew, through the mystery unravelled in Rom. 9.11; man and woman, in the relationship, also mysterious, of Christ and his Church; the slave and the free man, the one apprenticed to freedom and the other to service, through their belonging to the same Liberator; the civilized man and the Scythian, in the mutual discovery of a folly that confounds wisdom and of a wisdom that creates order.

'Christ is all, and in all' (or 'among all'). Col. 3.11, reciting the list again, draws this conclusion: it means that the Lord assumes and ensures for everyone his genuine personality, through his renewal in God's image. Far from opposing or neutralizing each other in their very different circumstances, baptized persons form

---

[20] Schweitzer, *Mysticism*, pp. 134f.; Bonnard, CNT X, *ad loc*. We must notice the eschatological nature of this image, in the same perspective as the eschatological nature of justification.

[21] It seems to us that Dibelius is wrong in talking of equality here (HNT 12, on Col. 3.10).

that new Man in whom the world's reconciliation, sealed on the cross, is realized.

It remains only to read the admirable parenesis that follows, to reveal its scope: 'As the Lord has forgiven you, so you also must forgive' (Col. 3.13), echoing Rom. 15.7, to which we finally come back: 'Welcome one another, therefore, as Christ has welcomed you, for the glory of God.' Jews and Gentiles, whose election together Paul has fathomed, and to whom he now returns, have all been received by the same grace of the Lord, who has shown God's faithfulness towards the circumcised, and his mercy towards the uncircumcised. And that faithfulness and that mercy, which form the texture of the divine wisdom, are now to be expressed in the brotherly welcome of the Christians of the capital. Divine grace means hands held out. The series of Old Testament references that follow expresses well the great theological significance that Paul attaches to this testimony; they bring out the great promises of the exaltation and glory of God among the nations.

When the bread is broken, Christ takes shape in his people; sharing the same bread, living on the same Lord, all are now one.[22] The drama of the church of Corinth, set out sorrowfully in chapter 11, arises from a misconception of this grace. Anxious to appropriate for themselves the virtues of the Eucharist, and greedy for spiritual power, the Corinthians, probably still influenced by certain mystical repasts, rush to the Lord's table to devour the food. By this they dishonour the body and blood of Christ—not that they have a sacrilegious attitude towards the bread or the cup, but because, being incapable of waiting for one another, they do not know how to receive God's gift there. In this they show that they have not yet learnt to discern the Lord's Body, i.e. to recognize it in one another.[23]

[22] See I Cor. 10 and 11.
[23] Traditional theology has distinguished three, if not four, forms of the Body of Christ: Jesus' physical body, his spiritual resurrected body, his eucharistic body, and his mystical Body, the Church. These distinctions, which are unknown to the New Testament, have weighed heavily on eucharistic and ecclesiological controversies. At present, the tendency of exegesis is towards identifying the spiritual and mystical Body (a first step) and also the spiritual and eucharistic body. When Paul mentions Christ's Body, even in the texts on the Lord's Supper, he is probably thinking, almost without exception, of the Church—some say with no exception at all. The latest study in this sense is that of E. Rietschel, 'Der Sinn des Abendmahls nach Paulus', *EvTH* 18, 1958, pp. 269ff.; but he refers to classical works: cf. W. G. Kümmel, HNT 9, p. 181; E. Schweizer, 'Forschungsbericht über das

Christianity According to Paul

Such is the unworthiness of the communion practised in Corinth, the guilt that kindles on them the fire of judgment whose effects they are already experiencing. By isolating themselves from each other for selfish profit, the Corinthians are isolating themselves from Christ. They no longer share the same bread, and the Body is thereby injured. The consequences are serious, coming back to them in the form of illness and death: if the Body is torn, the members are ill; if the Body lacks health, the members are dying. The Lord's Supper, indeed, is where the Spirit acts, where the power of the world to come strengthens, sustains, feeds each of the members, entering into them and renewing them in their physical as well as in their spiritual being.[24]

Belonging to Christ, therefore, concerns the whole man, not only his inner life, but equally his social, family, and conjugal existence, and still more closely, the functioning of his organs, his nervous and muscular poise. As we have seen, the physical being is not, any more than the inner being, definitely transformed thereby, but it does benefit, like the inner being, from the Spirit's work, while it awaits the ultimate resurrection.[25]

Thus, far from being an escape, sharing in the Lord's Supper brings involvement; far from taking us away from other people's presence, in so far as it is a bearer of Christ's presence it takes us into it. In Calvin's magnificent words, commenting on I Cor. 11, 'Lastly, where the faithful do not communicate among themselves, it is no use calling it the Lord's Supper.' Mutual respect, attention, welcome: these three very human gestures seem to be more than ever able here, round the Lord's table, to convey the miracle of his coming among his own.[26] The sacramental miracle is realized in

---

Herrenmahl im Neuen Testament', *TLZ* 2, 1954, pp. 577ff. See E. Brunner, *Dogmatics* II, ET, 1952, p. 376: 'When Paul speaks of the Body of Christ he means the Church, and nothing but the Church.'

[24] There is no magic here. See J. Héring's pertinent remark, CNT VII, *ad loc.*, p. 104 n. 1: 'Magic consists in influencing the supernatural by nature; here it is grace that is to come into the natural world.'

[25] See O. Cullmann, 'La délivrance anticipée du corps humain' in *Hommage et reconnaissance à K. Barth*, Neuchâtel, 1946, where all this is excellently set out. The practical consequences of these Pauline affirmations, for preaching or the cure of souls, deserve most careful consideration.

[26] We shall have occasion to come back once more to the ethical aspect of life in Christ. But we can already see here a forceful assertion of the specific nature of the Christian sacrament, which it receives from its origin, the redemptive event, and which never dissociates the moral from the mystical, the symbol from the actual. Cf. H. von Soden's acute study, *Sakrament und Ethik bei Paulus*.

the social miracle. The eucharist is, as it were, the visible demonstration of what was effected by baptism. The Lord's presence is celebrated by the cup of praise and in the broken bread in which we see the Church itself; where Jew and Greek, slave and free man, Scythian and barbarian become members one of another, where the brotherly circle is formed, there Christ is.

2. DEATH AND LIFE, SUFFERING AND COMFORT

'For me, to live is Christ. . . .' What has been said above is enough to give, from now on, a new dimension to the apostle's exclamation, and prevents it from ever being confined to the inner life. For him, being in Christ means that existence will henceforth be determined by others. Bultmann has shown, in his valuable analysis of Paul's view of the meaning of life, how justification, freeing man from distress, takes definite shape for him by opening out into the future in an existential freedom, giving, he says, quite new possibilities.[27] We were none the less surprised not to meet among the possibilities the effect of communion in Christ. The apostle has received freedom to live in the Lord, that is to say as a member of his body; in trying to find out how he finds himself affected by it, shall we not get a first-hand impression of this new existence?

Let us realize at once that, when he says that living for the Lord means living for others,[28] Paul does not mean that every moment must be given up to the concerns of his beloved converts, however movingly he may express himself in I Thess. 2.8, for instance. On the contrary, he writes a little farther on (I Thess. 3.8), 'For now we live, if you stand fast in the Lord.' Not merely, 'I am much relieved to know that you are behaving well. . . .' His own existence is in that of the Thessalonians; their faithful attachment to the Body of Christ gives him a renewal of life in the Lord, and enables him to pursue his work at Corinth with greater strength. We may quote II Cor. 7.3: '. . . . I said before that you are in our hearts, *to die and to live together (εἰς τὸ συναποθανεῖν καὶ συζῆν)*'. Here we could easily set out parallel quotations of pagan origin— the bond of life and death uniting the leader of the band and his

[27] *TWNT* II, pp. 868ff.
[28] Cf. the text of Rom. 14.7f. above.

acolytes, companions whose friendship is sealed *per fas et nefas*. But however eager he was, Paul does not invoke the only ties that he could have forged in his own heart.[29] He rather testifies to that specific communion that unites him in Christ to the Corinthians, a communion sealed in death to blossom out in life. For proof we want only the inversion that reverses this world's analogous expressions (living and dying together)[30] to give them the baptismal seal, the reality of death and life with Christ.[31]

Perhaps the most noteworthy text is II Cor. 4.11, 12: 'For while we live we are always being given up to death for Jesus' sake, so that the life of Jesus may be manifested in our mortal flesh. *So death is at work in us, but life in you.*' This takes us into the most mysterious sphere of these relationships, where life and death, but also sufferings and comfort, continually meet and interchange.

The theme of power and weakness will give us a first illustration. At the heart of the Christian condition there is the paradox of the preaching of the cross, 'folly to those who are perishing, but to us who are being saved it is the power of God'.[32] Such is God's sovereign choice, which nothing can or shall justify—least of all any complacent analysis of the value of weakness or suffering or poverty. The power of God was unfolded in his creation, but man laid hands on it to try to impose on other men[33]—and on God himself, whom man identifies with that power carried to its extreme limit. Thus God chose the weak things of the world— Israel, Paul and his preaching, the church at Corinth, and, at the centre, the cross of Jesus—to confound, to reveal himself as the Living One, the Wholly Other, to save. But the Corinthians, whose natural greed has been, as it were, aroused by the experi-

---

[29] In the same sense, H. Windisch, KEK 6, *ad loc.*

[30] According to Athenaeus, Nicolaus Damascenus characterizes the Ambacti, a people of Gaul, as συζῶντας καὶ συναποθανοῦντας. Horace, *Carmina* III, 9.24: *tecum vivere amem, tecum obeam libens* . . ., etc. (quotations in J. Héring, CNT VIII, *ad loc.*).

[31] Paul tells the Philippians that if he wants to remain in his body, in spite of his earnest wish 'to depart and be with Christ', it is 'for your progress and joy in the faith'. The companions that God has given him in Christ justify the continuance of his existence on earth and maintain his desire to live there.

[32] I Cor. 1.18. Bonnard's excellent study in *ETR*, 1958, pp. 61ff., makes it unnecessary for us to go into this more fully. He shows why and how this theme goes through the letters to the Corinthians from beginning to end. It is, moreover, intermingled with those of wisdom and folly, poverty and riches, where we could find, with the necessary shades of difference, the same dialectic and the same relationships.

[33] See the beginning of Romans.

ences that they have just undergone, can feel only the spiritual power that emanates from the preaching of the gospel. They think they have arrived. And it is here that their pastor's weakness comes in, with the weakness of his language: he is in the midst of the body, and with it, to signify the presence of the cross. Bonnard rightly speaks of that 'mysterious balance of strength and weakness right at the heart of the Church. The apostle has to be weak and despised there, so that the Corinthians can be filled with power, and so that joy can hold sway on both sides: "We are glad when we are weak and you are strong." The Church needs the permanent witness of God's weakness, side by side with the signs of strength. Christ risen is no substitute for Christ crucified. Paul sees both in the exercise of his ministry.'[34]

This throws light on II Cor. 10–13, and we may summarize their conclusion, in broad outline, as follows: 'You have received the power of God? Yes, quite true, Christ is not without strength among you, but as far as we are concerned, we are *weak in him*. The things that I heard in the third heaven cannot be uttered, but to make up for that, here is what the Lord said to me, for you as well as for me: "My grace is sufficient for you. . . ."[35] Do you compare the conditions of my service with the achievements of the other apostles, and seek a sign that Christ speaks through my weakness? *Find it in his power manifested in you!* Test yourselves. Do you not realize that Jesus Christ is in you? We are not trying to get the better of you, but to lead you to what is good, even if it were at the cost of our defeat, and to your loving us less while we love you the more. . . .' That is how the apostle puts it. In him the sign of the cross, in them that of the resurrection.[36] In these circumstances it is only reciprocal communion that can be a valid manifestation of the Lord's presence—the risen and the crucified Lord—among his own.[37]

---

[34] *Art. cit.*, p. 69.
[35] Cf. below, pp. 77f.
[36] II Cor. 13.4 may be interpreted in various ways. See *En Christ*, p. 46.
[37] It would be wrong to turn this into systematic teaching to determine who are the strong and the weak in a parish, or even to load the preacher with the burden of the cross so as to clothe the others in the garment of the paschal feast. Paul here leaves the particular facts of the Corinthian situation so as to get at its theological significance, and thus make his intervention effective. This is shown by P. Bonnard. Cf. also J. Héring: 'The apostle glories in this weakness, which is existential and is not to be confused with an attitude of weakness fashionable with certain pseudo-Paulinians' (*Le royaume de Dieu*, p. 237).

Christianity According to Paul

'As we share abundantly in Christ's sufferings, so through Christ we share abundantly in comfort too . . .' (II Cor. 1.5ff.). 'Now I rejoice in my sufferings for your sake, and in my flesh I complete what is lacking in Christ's afflictions for the sake of his body, that is, the church' (Col. 1.24), etc.

These texts take us as directly as does suffering itself to the apostle's heart. What was he experiencing, when he described his physical sufferings not as Paul's tribulations, but Christ's? Following so many others, we look over the edge of this mystery, not to dissect something that does not belong to us, but to find, in our turn, God's revelation. Following so many others . . . The studies are as numerous as they are divergent:[38] why should that surprise us, since here what is most personal in Paul's contribution joins what he received through tradition, since we are exactly at the cross-roads of Hellenist lines of thought, which are still under control but will burst forth later, and of Jewish theology, in particular that of martyrdom?

The trials that left their marks on the apostle's body, and so deeply affected his outlook as pastor, are as varied as the circumstances of his ministry, from Antioch to Philippi, from Ephesus to Jerusalem or Rome. Without on that account trying to reduce them to the same category, we can see that they are oriented round two poles, the two terms that he likes best to use when he wants to sum them up—*pathēma* and *thlipsis*. The former means 'passion' in the two senses of suffering and intense emotion.[39] In

---

[38] We may note here the principal ones: J. Schneider, *Die Passionsmystik des Paulus* (Untersuchungen NT 15), 1929. According to this, Paul developed a mystical theology feeding on Christ's passion, so as to summon the Church to do the same.

A. Schweitzer, *Mysticism*, ch. VII, pp. 141ff. We have already indicated the wealth of this chapter. Everything is illuminated if we start from the certainty: I have been crucified with Christ. Tribulations are the daily consequence and incessant manifestation of this certainty; and furthermore, they atone for sins committed after baptism.

T. Preiss, 'La mystique de l'imitation du Christ et de l'unité chez Ignace d'Antioche' in *La vie en Christ*, pp. 8ff. In pages full of spiritual meaning as well as theological insight, Preiss analyses, in relation to Paul's attitude, the flame of martyrdom that consumes the Bishop of Antioch.

G. Kittel, 'Col. 1.24' in *ZST*, 18, 1941, pp. 186–91. The disciples' tribulations are the reflection of those that Jesus underwent—not, however, the cross itself, but hatred, persecution, and contempt, which overtook the master before they reached the disciples. The apostolic tribulations are Christ's because he announced them from the beginning.

[39] In the sense of suffering undergone (e.g. what the woman with the haemorrhage suffered at the hands of the doctors, Mark 5.26; and the tragic fate of the Galileans

the New Testament as a whole it is generally reserved for the sufferings at Calvary, and the epistles use it essentially to characterize sufferings endured for the gospel (Acts 9.16; Phil. 1.29; I Thess. 2.14, etc.), sufferings ascribed to Christ himself (the believer's sufferings in Christ, Christ's sufferings in the believer). The great difficulty is to lay down exactly how far Paul joins them to the historical sufferings of the passion, or distinguishes between the cross and what Christ endures in his Body ('Saul, Saul, why do you persecute me?').

Thlipsis plays a rather more extensive part;[40] while approximating somewhat to 'distress', it gives the idea of clasping, squeezing, and compressing. Although it includes the most varied situations, it has a specific meaning associated with the torments and tribulations of Israel, especially those of the 'pious' who represent the 'remnant'. The 'pressures', all interconnected, at last form one single pressure which goes beyond personal afflictions or psychological agonies; towards its end it is as if through narrower and narrower defiles, or as if through the accelerating pangs of childbirth.

If in Jewish apocalyptic writings the great tribulation appears as a future threat, for the first Christians the perspectives of history have radically changed. The death and resurrection of Jesus, the turning-point of the world, have simultaneously set in motion the ultimate event and conquered death, which is the power of the *thlipsis*. The last days have come, there will be no more slackening in the rhythm of distress. But another change is working at the same time, completing an evolution that can already be seen in Judaism: the final curse has fallen on the Righteous One, and behind him it is not the unbelievers but the believers who will henceforth be most directly assailed. The Church finds itself as if

---

executed by Pilate, Luke 13.2—which shows how far this 'suffering' goes). In the sense of feelings that take possession of one's being and carry it along, as in Rom. 7.5; Gal. 5.24.

[40] Our translations render it by such differing terms that they disguise the thread of continuity. They work the opposite way to the LXX translators, who for their part had translated by the same word a great number of Hebrew terms describing various tribulations—a serious political situation, social oppression, slavery, danger of death, exile, war, prison, famine, persecutions, accidents, all become 'distresses', as does inward anguish. In connecting together such varied trials, the LXX testifies to the importance assumed by the idea of *thlipsis* in later Judaism, especially in the apocalyptic writings.

Christianity According to Paul

wedged in between the age to come, to which it belongs, and the present age, in which it is now living. Such is its mystery, for the Christian Church is the scene of the other eschatological event, the bestowal of the Spirit and the preaching of the gospel, which is its fruit and propagating seed. *Euangelion* and *thlipsis* go forward together; they are involved in each other, and can no more be separated in the epistles than can the Lord's cross and resurrection. The power of the world to come is already at work, and, by anticipation, is freeing life. The very bodies of church members are benefiting by its action, and inversely, as if putting the brake on, the *thlipsis* gets them in its grip. As to the nearness of the Kingdom, it is somewhat as with Einstein's mathematics, where space and time are no longer absolute uniform values, but relative to the point where one stands. So it is with the judgment of the world. The nearer we are to the Lord, the more we find ourselves involved in the final action.[41] The Church takes its place at the fiery centre of the conflict, and in its midst, in the front line, is the bearer of the gospel. Those on the periphery, still far from the Kingdom, escape its heat for a time (the shock will be all the fiercer when it comes). At the moment, no one is harder hit than the apostle. The further forward he goes, the more he runs, urged on by the Spirit, the more deeply he is involved in distress. Disciples or apostles, therefore, can also be clearly conscious of bearing tribulations in Christ's name, by virtue of their election and faith.[42] But they also know here and now the certainty of the *dénouement*: distress has come to have a different meaning for them. The

---

[41] As for example in martyrdom. See E. Loymeyer's noteworthy study, 'L'idée de martyre dans le judaïsme et dans le christianisme primitif' (*RHPR* VII, pp. 316–29). At the time of death, martyrdom is close to the parousia (e.g. the martyrdom of Stephen). Here, as in his commentaries on Philippians or Revelation, Lohmeyer seems to have been obsessed by this idea and by the presentiment of his own fate.

[42] Except for Col. 1.24 (which does not make its interpretation any easier), Christ's *thlipsis* is never mentioned. His παθήματα have, in a sense, marked the culminating point of tribulation, but henceforth he is Lord, master of time and also of tribulation, which no longer has the power to separate us from his love (Rom. 8.35). Seated at God's right hand, he is the sovereign judge to preside over the supreme trial, free to shorten its duration (Matt. 24.22). So, if he is involved in the *thlipsis*, it is only through his own people, his Body.

We are not comparing the words παθήματα and θλίψεις, even if they are closely connected and the apostle's παθήματα come from the *thlipsis* (inversely, cf. *TWNT*, Oepke, IV, p. 1091; Schlier, III, p. 143; Hauck, III, p. 806; W. Michaelis, V, 930). The most concise definition is Delling's (art. πληρόω, VI, p. 305 n. 3): 'θλίψεις in the NT denote not the sufferings of Jesus himself, but only the distresses which are the result of union with Christ.'

Communion in Christ

anguish, as maddening and inescapable as in one of Kafka's novels, has cleared away, and they know that they are on that narrow way that leads to life and emerges into the Reign. So, at the very time when they are in the grip of their ordeal, they can overcome it with perseverance, knowing that their struggle is not in vain in the Lord; more than that, they rejoice with glory and delight: Christ is the victor; he has emerged on the other side; tribulation gives them the measure of time; the end is approaching, and the slight momentary affliction is preparing for them an eternal weight of glory beyond all comparison.[43]

Paul never considers his own personal position apart from this vast context; if we individualize his situation by losing sight of the dimensions of the drama where his adventures take place, we are prevented from understanding him. His sufferings are Christ's, because they depend on his status as servant and envoy. But we must not be confused between what Luther called the *Knechtsleiden* and the *Herrenleiden*. The Lord's sufferings are accomplished once for all, and the matter is not to be reopened. They have fallen on the apostle, too, once for all, in baptism.[44] Christ's sufferings, which he will then bear, will be given him from day to day, all through his ministry, in obedience; they are not now those of the cross, but of the preaching of the cross, not those of Christ 'in the days of his flesh', but those of Christ in his Body which is the Church.

---

[43] We have no wish to multiply references, but we can hear the chords that this theme strikes across the New Testament literature. Thus:

The narrow way (Matt. 7.14, AV) is that of the *thlipsis*. This constitutes the trial through which God is continually purifying and sanctifying the Church, and fitting it for the reign that is coming. It is tested in its faithfulness (= by every test), but not condemned. Faith is made real in endurance (ὑπομονή), through the *thlipsis*, and endurance holds out to the end (cf. Rom. 5.3). Joy, a signal from the world to come, breaks out even in the midst of the *thlipsis*, since every tribulation brings with it the pains of childbirth and the time of release. Comfort, or, better, help (παράκλησις), is the intervention to provide company for one who is overtaken by tribulation; it assures him of a presence, a defence, and a hope. Relief (ἔνεσις) is a slackening of the *thlipsis*, an easing of the pressure, as, for example, was refused to Paul in Macedonia; God, however, will grant it as a just recompense to those who have faced interminable *thlipsis* (II Thess. 1.7).

For a list of the apostle's trials, cf. Schweitzer, *Mysticism*, pp. 147ff.

[44] See ch. II. Perhaps too little stress has been laid on the striking analogy between the story of Paul's conversion and the meaning that he gave to baptism. The meeting with the risen Lord was followed by three days' prostration, when Paul was as if buried, without eating or drinking. On the third day Ananias went and laid his hands on him, 'and immediately . . . he regained his sight. Then he rose and was baptized, and took food and was strengthened' (Acts 9.18–19).

Christianity According to Paul

This long detour enables us to bring new light to the passages that occasioned it.

We had already met with II Cor. 4.16ff., which here takes on another dimension. Paul does not recite his afflictions so as to unburden himself to the Corinthians; what he has in view is the ministry of the gospel, and this theme introduces that of tribulations. He has recourse to an unusual expression, *nekrōsis* (II Cor. 4.10), clearly distinguishing between that kind of death and the *thanatos* that baptism meant to him;[45] he had, as a matter of fact, already written to the same Corinthians, 'I die every day' (I Cor. 15.31), disclosing the effects of the Lord's hold on his life. Scars, weals from whipping, spiritual griefs, fevers arising from his care of the churches, stamp on his body the marks of Christ's death; but at the same time, if he carries on his ministry, Jesus' life will indeed triumph in his own flesh,[46] not in the final perspective of the resurrection, but from now on: 'Without taking our mortal flesh out of the process which ends in death, Jesus' life sustains it by a kind of continual miracle.'[47]

But the more personal aspect does not so much concern his own person and what happens to him; he understands it only in the light of that twofold mystery inseparable from the forward march of the Word and communion with the Church. Jesus' death, and through that his life, are literally expressed in the apostle's death and in his life, which are put down to Christ's account 'for his body, which is the Church'. The ordeal that comes down on the bearer of the gospel, ratifying his ministry, becomes the power of life for the Corinthians: 'So death is at work in us, but life in you' (II Cor. 4.12).

We must not deduce from this that the apostle attaches some redemptive value to his own ordeals, even if he bears them on Christ's account.[48] The texts in which, according to H. Windisch, Paul regards his sufferings as effective by substitution, are hardly

---

[45] Thus Bultmann, *TWNT* IV, art. νέκρωσις, rather than H. Windisch (KEK 6, *ad loc.*), according to whom Paul thereby understood his life as a permanent 'exposition' of Jesus' passion.

[46] It is noteworthy that the apostle writes here (II Cor. 4.11) of 'Jesus', the most human name that he can give to his Lord. Never do we approach nearer to the idea of an incarnation of Jesus in his own people. The absence of any reference to the *pneuma* in this passage is the more significant.

[47] J. Dupont, *L'union avec le Christ*, p. 125.

[48] 'Was Paul crucified for you?' (I Cor. 1.13).

Communion in Christ

conclusive.[49] Must we also seek an explanation in the disproportion between what the apostles had to endure and what the Corinthians have put up with? We do not think so.[50] We see in Phil. 1.12–14 the very practical way in which the imprisonment was able to contribute, in certain circumstances, to the gospel's progress and the building up of the Church. But here the apostle puts quite a different interpretation on a bond that has thus become apparent. It is not a cognitive bond, and we cannot weigh Paul's sufferings against the strengthening of his parishioners. In the intense struggle that he maintained in Ephesus, where death was hanging over him, the life of Christ shines in his threatened person with an intensity never known before, and at the same time it spreads to the whole body. The Corinthians, who hardly suspect the apostle's dramatic affliction, and may rather be said to accentuate it, are none the less its beneficiaries. Death (and in a sense the divided church in Corinth contributes to it) works in me, but through what unites us life is at work in you!

The development of the thought of the first chapter are similarly inspired; it is centred on the theme of affliction and comfort. Here again, the relationship that unites the Lord and the apostle is expressed in that which unites him to the Corinthians: sharing together in Christ's sufferings and comforts (II Cor. 1.7), they experience their mutual interplay: 'For as *we* share abundantly in Christ's sufferings *(παθήματα)*, so through Christ[51] *we* share abundantly in comfort too. If *we* are afflicted *(θλιβόμεθα)*, it is for *your* comfort and salvation;[52] and if *we* are comforted, it is for

---

[49] KEK 6, *ad loc.* Windisch quotes Col. 1.24; I Cor. 4.13; Rom. 9.3 (taken from quite a different context). . . . Paul's sufferings are not *substitutive* any more than he thinks of substituting himself for his Master. Nor are they expiatory. Strangely, Windisch does not quote Phil. 2.17: 'Even if I am to be poured as a libation upon the sacrificial offering of your faith, I am glad and rejoice with you all.' This text has given rise to a great deal of misconception. Cf. P. Bonnard, CNT X, *ad loc.* A libation is an offering poured out to accompany the main sacrifice, which is here the Philippians' faith. *A fortiori*, a libation is not an expiatory sacrifice. It is neither used up nor destroyed, but poured out, and the apostle's expression ought rather to be a reminder of his own life humbly given to water the sacrifice, the Philippians' faith (in this sense, see A. Butte, *Les offrandes sacrificielles dans le Nouveau Testament*, thesis, Montpellier, 1959). The ἀλλὰ εἰ καί, however, inclines us to think that Paul is here envisaging a hypothesis, that of his martyrdom (see Lohmeyer, KEK, *ad loc.*).

[50] H. Lietzmann has the merit of simplicity: 'My exhausting missionary work builds you up at the expense of my health!' (HNT, *ad loc.*).

[51] διὰ τοῦ χριστοῦ: through the intervention of the glorious Christ, intervening as Paraclete (cf. Lietzmann and Kümmel, HNT 9, p. 196).

[52] Here 'salvation' means perseverance up to the final deliverance; we find an analogous meaning in Col. 1.24.

your comfort, which you experience when you patiently endure the same sufferings that *we* suffer. *Our* hope for *you* is unshaken, for we know that as you share in our sufferings, you will also share in our comfort' (vv. 5–7). The common idea that the only people who can comfort others are those who have undergone the same trials does not do justice to the text. The source of comfort is not that Paul and the Corinthians can sympathize with each other through experience and by feeling a certain relief in return: it comes from God, and Paul has received it simply in order to share it—or rather, he receives it by sharing it (v. 4). On the other hand, it is too much to say that he mediates it; such an interpretation moves away from the reality that is revealed here of reciprocal communication in Christ.[53] The sufferings that Paul brings to mind are again the great tribulation that came upon him in Asia, where he despaired of life. He hung between life and death, and the vicissitudes of the struggle, which can still be felt in his manner of writing, culminate, as do the tense dilemmas of the epistles, in a shout of victory. As the apostle's struggle was Christ's (we remember the bond that the Hebrew mind forges between the envoy and his master), it provided the Church with comfort in proportion to the ordeal. How can we not be alive to the surprising transpositions of possessive adjectives or personal pronouns that mark line after line of the passage? It needs all Christ's power for these sentences not to sound rhetorical, but to express in unforgettable accents of truth the communion of the members of the Body *in Christo*.

'If one member suffers, all suffer together; if one member is honoured, all rejoice together' (I Cor. 12.26). This assertion, which is repeated so often, and sometimes to so little purpose, is therefore explained, not in the sense of mutual sympathy or mutual congratulation, but by the communication that the Holy Spirit establishes among all those who have been baptized into the one single Body. Thus so-and-so's trials, without any alteration in their actual character, cease to be exclusively so-and-so's, and become those of the members—that is, those of Christ.[54]

[53] H. Windisch talks of an apostolic mediation in comfort, as he had talked of Paul's substitutive suffering. KEK 6, *ad loc.*

[54] This follows literally from v. 12, at least if we understand it rightly: 'For just as the body is one and has many members, and all the members of the body, though many, are one body, so it is with Christ.'

Communion in Christ

But we still have to question the most enigmatical of the texts, viz. Col. 1.24:[55] the extreme terseness of the passage makes the interpretation difficult. It is dominated by three problems:[56]

(*a*) This is the only passage that mentions Christ's θλίψεις. We can understand them as referring to Jesus' historical sufferings, which are continued in the specific tribulations of the apostolate;[57] we can also see in them the tribulations experienced by Christ in his members, in particular by the apostles (in the former case the tribulations follow from the apostolate, and in the latter case from baptism).

(*b*) 'In my flesh' can refer either to the verb 'complete' or to 'Christ's afflictions', and we then get two quite different translations.[58]

(*c*) Two rare words, ἀνταναπληρόω and ὑστερήματα, also present difficulties. The former implies reciprocity,[59] not in the perspective of redemptive substitution, but in that (which we have already partly seen) of communal sharing in which one can live, suffer, and stand fast for the benefit of another (or others). ὑστερήματα sets

---

[55] As far as possible, we leave aside here the problems raised by this verse which are peculiar to Colossians—as, for example, the possible echoes of the word πληρόω in a milieu where the pleroma plays such a part, or again, the speculations on the cosmic body which here compel the apostle to specify 'his body, that is, the church'.

[56] See p. 76 n. 42 for references to the principal treatments in *TWNT*; see, too, p. 74 n. 38 for a brief bibliographical summary. We must add the commentaries on Colossians, and an article by M. Carrez, 'Souffrance et glorie dans les épîtres pauliniennes', *RHPR* 31, 1951, pp. 343–43; the translation used at the end does not satisfy us, as it assumes an individual perspective that is foreign to the sense of the θλίψις: 'I endure to the full what remains for me to suffer through the presence of Jesus Christ in my flesh, for his body. . . .'

[57] Of the apostolate only. That is the interpretation of C. Masson (CNT X, *ad loc.*), who finds support from Haupt, Schlatter, Percy, and Rendtorff. But in that case, one has to force the meaning of the word θλίψεις and make it the equivalent of παθήματα. Moreover, Masson's objection does not seem to us convincing. If, he says, it were a question of Christ's tribulations, undergone by himself in his members, how could Paul then declare that they are endured for that Body? But cannot one member of the Body suffer for the good of the others?

[58] (1) 'In my flesh I complete what is lacking in Christ's afflictions for the sake of his body, that is, the church' (RSV). (2) 'I . . . fill up on my part that which is lacking of the afflictions of Christ in my flesh for his body's sake, which is the church' (RV).

[59] The prefix ἀντ- can mean 'in my turn', and this suggests another idea. It is the meaning adopted by M. Carrez. But it can just as well indicate the idea of exchange—which we prefer, with Delling (*TWNT* VI, p. 305, πληρόω, ἀνταναπληρόω): 'Here the prevailing idea is that of substitutionary filling up, and particularly of the sum total of the eschatological tribulations, which are inflicted on the Church in a sharing in Christ's sufferings which is not mystical but quite real and actual, and is based on dying with him.'

Christianity According to Paul

us a different problem, this time not philological but theological.[60] If the want that is to be suffered concerns the apostle, the meaning is simple: it is a question of what he will have to endure till the end of his course. But if it refers to the sum total of afflictions which are to oppress the Church, does Paul then suppose that a certain *mass* of eschatological sufferings may have to be endured to the end, and that he will have to bear the burden of it? This idea, which is rather disconcerting for our modern minds, must not be set aside *a priori*,[61] though, of course, one would not introduce any idea of strict accountancy.

It seems, then, that every word of this verse is pointed; and the paths leading from it ramify continually. If we must try to trace its course, we are inclined to think that it is a question here of eschatological tribulations, set in motion by the cross, which Christ undergoes in his Body, and of which Paul, as apostle to the Gentiles and minister of the gospel, must take his full share[62] for the benefit of the Church. Such, at least, is the orientation that seems to be given to this inexhaustible verse by a context which, unfortunately, has never been given enough attention. From the point of view of the vocabulary, the links in the chain of words are strikingly obvious—'in his body of flesh' (v. 22); 'in my flesh ... for the sake of his body' (v. 24); ἀνταναπληρόω and πληρῶσαι (v. 25). . . .

Verse 24 is, in fact, put into a closely woven argument, which is in

---

[60] The meaning of this, as of the previous word, is well analysed by M. Carrez, *art. cit.* Unfortunately he does not tackle the problem fundamentally. In general it is translated by 'what is lacking', 'remainder', 'residue'.

[61] It is found in Oepke, Delling (*TWNT, art. cit.* on p. 76 n. 42). For the opposite view see W. Michaelis (*id.*). The idea is not as absent as Michaelis supposes, either in the Hellenistic world or in Judaism. To quote R. Idi: 'The tribulations are divided into three parts. One third was borne by the fathers and the generations that followed them, one by the generation of the persecutions (under Hadrian). The last third will be borne by the Messiah.' In apocalyptic texts reference is often made to the number of days of the trials that are to be undergone. That number may be shortened (Matt. 24.22). In Acts the warning comes twice that Paul will have *much* to suffer in order to reach the Kingdom (9.16: 'I will show him how much he must suffer for the sake of my name'; cf. 14.22).

[62] One might even feel this conclusion is extended still further in the perspective of Paul's apostolic consciousness. Cf. O. Cullmann, 'Le caractère eschatologique du devoir missionnaire et la conscience apostolique de saint Paul' (*RHPR* 16, 1936, pp. 210–45). Even if we do not adopt the bold hypothesis according to which Paul identifies himself with the κατέχων of II Thess. 2.6, 7, we may admit that in so far as he was convinced of having been called to take the gospel to the Gentiles, as far as the ends of the earth, and thus to open the way to Christ's coming in glory, he was, by the same token, certain of having to take in full the rest of the θλίψεις. ὑστερήματα would be in some way associated with the idea of the κατέχον.

a way more fully developed by Eph. 2.11ff. After the hymn celebrating the supreme excellence of Christ, we have the mystery of his presence, the Church, which is meant to be the ultimate sign offered to men, as opposed to the powers, of 'the manifold wisdom of God' which is 'to unite all things in him'. And here the apostle brings out the final phases of God's plan, and says what place the Colossians will have there, and what part he himself is to play. He addresses the Colossians as those whom the gospel has rescued from paganism; they have been brought into the Body of Christ where the reconciliation of the Gentiles and of Israel has been sealed by the sacrifice of the cross (v. 22), where the 'new man' presages the Kingdom, where the 'mystery'[63] is at last revealed, Christ's presence in them and among them, Gentiles by birth, 'the hope of glory, for all creation (v. 27).

As far as Paul is concerned, he is called on in this final stage, 'according to the divine office which was given me for you, to make the word of God fully known' (v. 25); this is to be understood in a sense both extensive (making it known to the last Gentile) and intensive ('that we may present every man mature in Christ', v. 28).[64] The apostle therefore rejoices in the sufferings that he endures for them; if they have a purpose, it is not now the redemption that has been obtained (by Christ 'in his body of flesh'), but the completion of the plan of salvation (in my flesh . . . for the sake of his body'); and if there is anything lacking in the tribulations of Christ, it is not those of the cross, but those that are attached to the office of making 'the word of God fully known': the *thlipsis* goes with the *euangelion* up to the end. Such is the meaning of the apostolic sufferings, which complete, though they do not replace, the redemptive sufferings.[65] Christ bore the

[63] Paul always connects the term with the divine economy (see my article 'Mystery' in *VB*).

[64] This expression has a distinctly sacerdotal ring. The apostle's mission implies his priesthood. It is remarkable to find this vocabulary, both here, where it is a question of carrying the Word, of its completion in the intensive sense (presenting to God the Colossians who have become 'mature in Christ'), and also in the extensive sense (as in Rom. 15.10, where the apostle proclaims the gospel to the Gentiles so as to offer them to God). We find 'I have fully preached the gospel of Christ' in Rom. 15.19. J. Munck has studied this meaning at considerable length in his work *Paulus und die Heilsgeschichte*, 1954 (ET, *Paul and the Salvation of Mankind*, 1959).

[65] In line with what has been said above, we may wonder whether the prefix ἀντανα- might not refer to the πληρῶσαι of v. 25; we again find the binomial *euangelion-thlipsis*. Commissioned to proclaim the Word up to the last, Paul would be reciprocally (ἀντανα-) commissioned to draw, right to the last, the balance of the

latter on the cross; he assumes the former, in his apostle, for the benefit of the whole Body. Thus the *agōnia* that Paul expresses at the beginning of chapter 2[66] has the effect of setting the Colossians on the way to the illuminating discovery of the glorious riches of the mystery that has been revealed to them—Christ in us, the hope of glory.[67]

3. AGAPĒ

In the course of this chapter we have seen the personal relationship with the Lord take shape in mutual communion, and then, across the lines of Pauline antitheses, express, on the Church's level, the paradox that we had already found at the heart of the Christian condition, that which marks the biblical revelation and bears the imprint of Christ dead and raised again for us. But we cannot remain in dialectical tensions. If these are to be resolved one day, we must be able to foreshadow it somewhere; if Christ is Lord, his reign must be shown by a real pacification now. Where should adoration be possible? The mystery of salvation has its *dénouement*; thus, beyond the oppositions, the 'already' and the 'not yet', beyond Good Friday and Easter, election and rejection, the epistles show us clearly God's supreme gift, revealing the unity of all his work—*agapē*.

Life in Christ is a life in love; all the preceding pages witness to it as if in anticipation, though without as yet naming it; and those that follow will try to acknowledge it more explicitly.

In the epistles, God's love is not tied to any speculation resting on a previous conception of the divine nature.[68] According to biblical

---

thlipsis! Moreover, this would be the only interpretation to do the text full justice; the apostle, in fact, wrote τὰ ὑστερήματα, meaning all that is lacking, and not part of what is lacking. This interpretation would exactly correspond to Munck's conclusions on the place that Paul allotted himself in God's plan. It is a pity that Munck's suspicions with regard to Colossians-Ephesians prevent him from tackling these texts.

[66] Cf. Gal. 4.19, which uses another figure to indicate the same reality: 'My little children, with whom I am again in travail until Christ be formed in you.'

[67] We have a parallel text in Eph. 3.13, which again brings out the mystery of the relationship that unites the apostle and his converts: 'So I ask you not to lose heart over what I am suffering for you, which is your glory.'

[68] Theologians seem sometimes to be held back here by a singular reticence, wrongly thinking, perhaps, that they are being misled by sentiment. Cf. R. Bultmann's strange and significant silence at this point, with only a few lines in the whole of his *Theology of the New Testament*. There is compensation for this in P. Spicq's ample

perspectives, being is realized in action, and only his saving acts bring us to a direct knowledge of the living God. Thus God's *agapē* is an event.[69] The two great Pauline debates that gravitate round the world's redemption lead to an assertion that has been the immovable foundation of Christian thought—the act that justifies us, thanks to which we are freed, is the initiative of divine love:[70] 'The life I now live in the flesh I live by faith in the Son of God, who loved [aorist] me and gave himself for me' (Gal. 2.20); 'God shows his love for us in that while we were yet sinners Christ died for us' (Rom. 5.8).[71] God's love, then, found in the cross not only expression but also fulfilment.[72]

This historical fulfilment, moreover, is matched by an eschatological fulfilment which forms the bright horizon of the Pauline landscape. The world to come is that of fulness and perfection, because it is there that God's love will at last find its complete answer in the new creature, its free deployment in the new creation. That is the meaning of I Corinthians 13.[73]

This hymn fits into the epistle's themes so exactly, and is so

---

and scrupulous study, *Agapé dans le Nouveau Testament*, analyse des textes (3 vols, Paris, 1958–9). One of the most suggestive analyses is Albert Schweitzer's (*Mysticism*, pp. 303–7); it leads to a perspective perhaps more Johannine than Pauline, but it firmly establishes the permanence of love. E. Stauffer's article in *TWNT* (ET, *Love* [Bible Key Words 1], 1949), belongs to the earlier period of the *Wörterbuch*, when conciseness was insisted upon; but it gets down to essentials, just as does P. Bonnard's in *VB*.

[69] It would be difficult to overvalue the dogmatic or ethical consequences of this. See Cullmann, *Christ and Time*, ET, rev. ed., 1962, pp. 222ff.

[70] To Paul, *agapē* is God's love and Christ's love, which are inseparable; it is revealed in the cross, where the emphasis may be put on the Father's gift (Rom. 8.32) as well as on the Son's sacrifice (Gal. 2.20; Eph. 5.2).

[71] Here Paul's witness joins with that of John and the synoptists in asserting plainly the initiative of grace as characteristic of the divine love, which goes out to meet enemies with reconciliation (Rom. 5.10), to meet sinners with forgiveness (Luke 5.31, 32), to meet unloving people with love (I John 4.10).

[72] συνίστησιν τὴν ἑαυτοῦ ἀγάπην.... 'God shows his love for us' (RSV); 'That is God's own proof of his love towards us' (NEB). The verb's primary meaning suggests the idea of gathering together. God's action does not merely reveal his love; it constitutes it. On the variants of vv. 5 and 8 cf. Lietzmann, HNT 8, *ad loc*.

The Pauline aorist is very expressive, e.g. in II Thess. 2.16, 'who loved us'. Not that God's love belongs henceforth to the past, but because, if one may put it so, it took shape at a certain moment.

On the connection between God's love and 'for us', see Eph. 5.2.

[73] It is surprising that such responsible translations as the *Centenaire* or the Jerusalem Bible stick to the word '*charité*' here. This has the effect of introducing a hiatus between the love to which God bore witness on the cross, the love through which we love every day, and the love that remains everlastingly. One could hardly do a greater injustice to Paul's thought than by thus detaching brotherly love from divine love, and thereby separating what he had so closely joined.

entirely in line with the development of its thought, that it could not, as some have supposed, have been introduced here from somewhere else. We are at the heart of the letter, in the revelation of Christ as the Body of which the Corinthians are the members. Then follows the description of the different organs that are equally necessary for the life of this Body; the ministries are derived from the various gifts that are granted to the Church by the riches of God's grace and the outpouring of the Spirit. But these gifts could not bring about secession within the Church, for the golden rule formulated by the apostle is 'Let all things be done for edification' (14.26). Far from creating competition and and an outbreak of individualism, the *charismata* are sent to quicken the whole body and to strengthen it in its calling. Whatever their variety, and sometimes even their mystery, they are of the same character, they have a common denominator which relates them to each other, and makes each of them a grace to the profit of all—and that common feature, that constituent, is love. The first part of the hymn carries us away, with Paul, towards what might seem to be the pinnacle of the life of the Spirit. Each verse takes us a step higher, to discover at every stage of the ascent that the plateau reached is nothing but an empty desert if we do not meet *agapē* there. Still more: without love, all the *charismata* melt away, as if reduced to a state of paganism. Such is the 'more excellent way', that is, the common way for everyone; such we may say, is, the criterion by which we can judge the genuineness of gifts and spirits. As soon as we wander from this way, even the most spectacular manifestations leave the path of truth, separate from the body to join forces in a psychological explosion, in an effervescence not derived from Jesus Christ—holiness has deserted them. And why has love this primacy? The last verse tells us clearly: love is what abides, the absolute, in relation to which everything is relative; the eternal, as opposed to which everything is transitory. Faith itself will give way to sight, hope will be turned into possession when the inheritance is recovered: for us these are pilgrims' staffs,[74] but love is the goal of

---

[74] It may surprise us to see again in v. 13 the triad of faith, hope, and love, which seems to weaken the preceding development, as if the force of an expression already coined (I Thess. 1.3; 3.5) had made the apostle's pen outrun his thought. Moreover, the end of the verse seems to bring a final corrective to put love back on its different level (cf. E. Stauffer, *TWNT* I, art. ἀγάπη, p. 52; ET, *Love*, pp. 59f.).

the pilgrimage, already belonging to eternity, and forming whatever we can from now onwards know and enjoy of the Kingdom in which it will be unfolded without limit; then we shall see face to face, and understand fully, even as we have been fully understood.[75] *Agapē* is the beginning and the end of life *in Christo*, as it is the beginning and the end of the life of Christ.

Two passages bring together most forcibly that beginning and that end between which we are placed and told to live and to love: those of Eph. 3.14–21 and Rom. 8.31–39. In the former, the author asks that, with Christ's presence initiating us into God's love, we may be 'rooted and grounded in love' (and this sends us back to the foundation laid once for all), to go on towards its complete discovery, and to know what goes beyond all *gnosis*, the real dimensions of the *agapē* that embraces time and space.[76] The apostle's triumphant tones ring through the end of Rom. 8, and set us again on the magnificent heights of the final scene of God's plan. The actors are there again for the last time. Paul has just unfolded the *ordo salutis*, and with these sublime thoughts he reaches the final assurance: here, too, everything proceeds from the cross on which God has delivered his own Son for us. In it we have a pledge and a promise that he will 'give us all things with him' (v. 32). Faced by the enemy, temptations, hardships, and powers of every rank, the apostle defies them all; nothing will ever be able to separate him 'from the love of God in Christ Jesus our Lord'.[77] Since the year 29 the reality of the world to come has been present with us!

Thus *agapē* appears as the supreme gift of the Spirit. The Holy Spirit, which itself represents the guarantee of the future age, cannot more effectively make us anticipate the Kingdom than by causing us to share in the love of Christ. Before everything else, love is 'the fruit of the Spirit' (Gal. 5.22); the Spirit produces love (Rom. 15.30); 'God's love has been poured into our hearts through

---

[75] Cf. I Cor. 8.3 with its Johannine ring: 'If one loves God, one is known by him.'

[76] In v. 18 the dimensions are given different connections: with the heavenly inheritance (a prayer begun in 1.17); God's redemptive plan (the subject of ch. 3); love, as we think; cf. Masson, CNT, 1953, *ad loc*.

[77] Paul describes 'the three concentric circles which together show the reader the dramatic nature of the Christian condition', F. J. Leenhardt, CNT, 1957, *ad loc*. The three circles are those of the inward struggles of faith, the threats implemented by men, and the world's mysterious forces which escape all human control.

Christianity According to Paul

the Holy Spirit which has been given to us' (Rom. 5.5).[78] Thanks to the Spirit, God's love becomes the genuine reality of our present time, the content of the new life, at the heart of the new covenant. 'Love is the fulfilling of the law' (Rom. 13.8–10; Gal. 5.14); it 'builds up' (I Cor. 8.1; cf. Eph. 4.16); it is 'the bond of perfectness' (Col. 3.14, AV);[79] it is the motive force that quickens life in Christ (cf. Gal. 5.6), the power that has taken hold of the apostle and henceforth allows him no respite (II Cor. 5.14).

'Let all that you do be done in love' (I Cor. 16.14). We may say that if the Body of Christ is the present reality of the world to come, it is because, from now on, love is its constituent element. So we shall not be surprised to see *agapē* characterize relationships within the Christian community. Orders, injunctions, promises multiply in this sphere: I Thess. 4.9, 'You yourselves have been taught by God to love one another'; I Thess. 3.12; Philemon 5; Gal. 5.13; Eph. 1.15; Col. 1.4. . . . Because of Christ, it is the only debt that we have in relation to each other, since in this matter we are for ever debtors, and all that Christ has is in a way deposited on our neighbour's account (Rom. 13.8).

So we again see the question looming up that we suggested before: Can it be that this love assumes an exclusive character? It seems, in fact, that the apostle's requirements keep to brotherly love, within the Church. Here and there he chances to allude to those outside, but he puts it rather vaguely: in I Thess. 3.12 ἀλλήλους is followed by an indefinite 'to all men', and in Gal. 6.10 we read 'Let us do good to all men, and especially to those who are

---

[78] If Rom. 5.5 is thus understood, it corresponds quite well to the context in which love is the culmination of the progressive series sufferings/endurance, endurance/character, character/hope—hope which cannot deceive us, as we have already received the first instalments of it through the love that the Spirit has poured into our hearts. It is from the point of view of form that the verse presents difficulty: the expression 'love poured into our hearts' is rather strange. M. Dibelius proposes to transpose the terms: ' "Poured" is said with reference to love, but thought of with reference to the Spirit.' So we should have to interpret thus: 'Hope does not deceive us, because, through the Spirit that has been poured into our hearts, God's love has been pledged to us.' This interpretation slightly changes the emphasis of the last phrase, but it has the advantage of taking better account of the verb ἐκκέχυται (M. Dibeleius, *Vier Worte des Römerbriefes* [Symbolae Biblicae Upsalienses 3], Uppsala, 1944, pp. 3–6).

[79] This 'bond of perfectness' has been understood in quite different ways; see Masson, CNT X, p. 146 n. 7. There might well be here an echo of I Cor. 13. Without love, the body disintegrates; and this applies both to the 'virtues' that characterize it (kindness, humility, meekness, patience, etc.) and to the persons who are its members.

Communion in Christ

of the household of faith.' Might there be here some instinctive transposition from the bond of the covenant in Israel to the bond of brotherhood in the Church?[80] Might it be that obedience to the commandment to love one's neighbour, which characterizes the Bible in contrast to all discarnate humanism, has perforce been turned towards the most immediate neighbours, namely 'those who are of the household of faith'?[81] It is possible to think of other suggestions. But the key seems to be the idea of *election*. Attention has been drawn to the equivalence that seems to exist between 'God's beloved' and 'God's chosen ones' (Rom. 1.7; Col. 3.12; II Thess. 2.13, etc.);[82] in the same way there is a latent synonymity between elect, saints, brothers, and well-beloved (e.g. I Thess. 2.8; Philemon 16). In fact, to connect it with election is to free this love from all exclusiveness, and to bring it into God's plan for the salvation of the nations; this is a matter of the Church's calling and destiny. *Agapē* does not close in on itself; it is centred in the Church's *koinōnia* to become at the same time a liturgy and a sign accompanying the message, the service of God and of the world.

God's love is seen in mutual love. We have stressed how important it is to keep the same word here, as it is a question of a divine reality that becomes human, with neither separation nor confusion. Some people separate them by calling one 'love' and the other 'charity'; others confuse them by turning human *eros* into *agapē*; others again—and we may put forward this objection with reference to A. Nygren, who saw the other dangers so clearly— make *agapē* so discarnate that it is difficult to see how that 'love' can either strengthen or hold us. We find here one of those vital links which, in spite of appearances, connect the Pauline and Johannine outlook. Where Paul had made a rough sketch as circumstances permitted, John gives us a finished design: 'Love one another as I have loved you.'[83] There have been long arguments about Johannine exclusivism,[84] but such arguments mistake

[80] E. Stauffer suggests this in *TWNT* I, p. 51 (ET, *Love*, p. 58).
[81] P. Bonnard suggests this in CNT IX, on Gal. 6.10.
[82] See the story of Jesus' baptism. Cf. O. Cullmann, *Christology of the New Testament*, p. 66. Matt. 12.18 translates the *bachir* of Isa. 42 by 'beloved', the Septuagint by 'elected'.
[83] John 15.12. The καθώς echoes the καθὼς καί of Rom. 15.7, which we have already met: 'Welcome one another, therefore, as Christ has welcomed you.'
[84] There is a good restatement in O. Prunet, *La morale chrétienne d'après le Quatrième Evangile*, Paris, 1957, pp. 107–15.

what the author intended to convey. The disciples' mutual love is the subject of Christ's culminating prayer, because he regards it as being of conclusive importance. With extraordinary daring, Jesus entrusts to this mutual fellowship the task, which he himself had not been able to achieve, of convincing the world by revealing to it his own divinity ('so that the world may believe that thou has sent me'). Just as Christ appeared for his own people as the *sēmeion* of the Father's love, so the disciples' mutual love was to appear for the world. If Jesus centres his fervent prayer on them, it is not in order to exclude other men, but to bring them, in their turn, to his light.

Now that we have reached the end of a chapter in which the various themes have not always been given their exact proportions, we hope that the reader has not been left with distorted ideas about communion in Christ, and that no morbid impression has been given, for instance, by our having spent longer on the theme of sufferings than on that of joy! These few analyses were, in fact, outlined only by way of example; one could fill in other features, or scrutinize the material afresh; but it seems legitimate to set out the conclusions that have emerged:

(*a*) In Christ the communication of individuals is restored, and at the same time man discovers his real condition. It is not a question of a nature that is to be perfected; he is a being who shares, and his real dimensions are not individual, but communal: 'Paul becomes another man with, through, and for other people.'[85]

(*b*) Mutual relationships belong, not to the *bene esse*, but to the *esse* of life in Christ. The most personal relationship with the Lord needs my neighbour in order that I may discover, reveal, and strengthen myself. As Bonhoeffer rightly said, 'The Christ whom we bear in our own hearts is weaker than the Christ who is brought to us by the Word', than the Christ who comes to us in the person of our brothers.

(*c*) Sharing in Christ is sharing in one another. It is in that relationship of union, realized through the Spirit from baptism onwards and renewed through the Lord's Supper, that the life of the Body of Christ is shown.

---

[85] Cf. H. Hatzfeld, *Traits généraux et problèmes particuliers de la morale paulinienne*, typewritten thesis, Strasbourg, 1947.

Communion in Christ

(*d*) In Christ, the Spirit is at work to carry out the redemptive plan. The realization of this plan is in no way a natural and progressive process; it calls into action the relationships and decisions of the church members, and it is on a level with the believer's daily obedience. The historical character of salvation has fixed for all time its ethical character by rejecting gnostic mirages. The Body of Christ exists for the sake of the Kingdom, and we shall try in the last chapter to state the connections between the Church and the new creation.

IV

LIFE IN CHRIST AND A NEW CREATION

1. THE BODY OF CHRIST AND A NEW CREATION

LOVE, then, as the constituent element of the Body of Christ and the fruit of the Spirit, points to the Church as a foreshadowing of the world to come. The title of this chapter is not meant to suggest that life in Christ and the new creation are the same thing; but it does suggest to us the theme of their relationship, on which Pauline ethics are based. It is significant that we are in touch here both with the latter end of *in Christo* and with the daily problems with which faith was confronted from the beginning, through the Church's existence in a pagan world.

We must notice at the outset that Paul does not use the expression 'new creation'. We meet only two passages that concern the 'new creature': Gal. 6.15 and II Cor. 5.17. First, we read in Gal. 6.15, 'Neither circumcision counts for anything, nor uncircumcision; but [it is a question of being] a new creature'.[1] The context establishes indisputably that by κτίσις Paul means here not 'creation' but 'creature'. Taking up again for the last time the theme of his letter, the apostle recalls that the régime of law has been succeeded by that of faith. The decisions about circumcision have resulted in a revolutionary situation—no other glory than the cross of Christ, through which the world is crucified for Paul, and Paul for the world; this attitude, rather than any moral perfection, marks the new creature who has entered into a new relationship with God and with the world. If we put this side by side with Gal. 5.6 ('For in Christ Jesus neither circumcision nor uncircumcision is of any avail, but faith working through love'), we find that an equivalent expression, 'faith working through love', has also been substituted for the superseded sign of circumcision. For the apostle, then, it was a question of stating the condition

---

[1] RSV and NEB both have 'a new creation'. Translator.

Life in Christ and a New Creation

for the believer, and not of appealing, at this stage, to the new creation.[2]

Might not this be the case in II Cor. 5.17? Many people have thought so in view of this text, which is one of the most fascinating of all that the apostle wrote. The spirit that inspires it might well prompt one to give it the widest possible range, whether in the first part of the verse, by understanding 'If anyone is in Christ, a new creation is there',[3] or by translating with J. Héring, 'The old world has passed away, and see, a new world has arisen.'[4]

May not the context point in this direction? As we have seen, this tense letter bears the marks of the difficulties that have arisen between the Corinthians and the apostle. The latter is out to reestablish his disputed authority, in support of which he makes the highest claims for his ministry and gospel. One verb recurs persistently: συνιστάναι, to commend or accredit.[5] It obviously concerns Paul's authority, the authority that he inspires and is acknowledged to possess, and finally, his relations with the members of the Church. The answer to the questions raised by his ministry is to be found neither in him nor in his converts. Where are we to look for the key? Where but in the letter itself and in what it sets out—an unadulterated gospel, a straightforward attitude, and primarily that love of Christ that lays hold of us, and opens the way to a real understanding of the world and also of individuals? The scope of Jesus' death is incalculable; all have received an incurable wound; all are dead,[6] and the world will not recover. Those who live (in Christ) can no longer live for themselves; not

---

[2] We do not follow A. Oepke when, in explanation of Gal. 6.15, he writes in THKNT IX, 'The new creation appears whenever anyone is in the new sphere of salvation (*Heilsregion*)—Christ!' Not only does the apostle not envisage here creation in general, but the previous chapter, too, gives us the more reason for not accepting a local conception of *in Christo*.

[3] To get this meaning, the grammatical construction has to be forced: 'if anyone is in Christ' becomes literally 'for whoever is in Christ'.

[4] J. Héring wisely dismisses the 'all' inserted by some MSS in v. 17 (CNT VIII, *ad loc.*).

[5] II Cor. 3.1; 4.2; 5.12; 6.4; 7.11; 10.12–18; 12.11.

[6] J. Héring's interpretation (CNT VIII) seems to be a misunderstanding; 14b is not now the consequence of 14a, but is presented as an objection to the affirmation of faith. So we must bend the meaning of ἄρα, which assumes an adversative value (Héring translates 'however') instead of its normal, consecutive meaning (cf. Blass, 451d).

We also cramp Paul's thought if we confine the 'all' to baptized people.

all have attained to that life, and yet henceforth we know no one after the flesh[7]—are we not with Christ himself in a different relationship, one that allows us to know him as Lord and brings us right into a new understanding of beings κατὰ Χριστόν?[8] If anyone is in Christ, he is a new creature; the old things have passed away, new ones have come. And all this comes from God, who has reconciled us to himself through Christ.

However great the scope of this passage and the force of its impact, we must not let ourselves be carried away beyond what Paul puts forward; the bigger the stake, the more we need to be sober. The full repercussion of Christ's death is already here, but obviously the same is not true of his resurrection. Once more, on the cosmic plane, we face the fundamental dissymetry that we have already noticed in Romans 6. In verse 17 the presence of the definite article to introduce 'the old things', and its absence before 'new', are extremely significant, as is also the harmonizing variant 'all things are new' rejected by Héring; this variant aims at creating a parallelism which the apostle has not confirmed, basically analogous to that which has taken the place of the early form of Romans 6 in the expression 'dead and raised with Christ'.[9]

So we cannot introduce the new creation here. When the new world comes, indeed, there will be no restriction, nor anything conditional; there will no longer be an 'if', unless it were 'if anyone is in Christ . . .' This confirms P. H. Menoud's pertinent note on J. Héring's commentary. He writes, 'According to Paul, the categories "old" and "new" are applicable only to the new creature; the apostle never speaks of an old world and a new world, but of a present world and a world to come, because for him the transition from one world to the other will take place only at the parousia.'[10] It is possible to punctuate verse 17 in different

---

[7] Even those who are still living after the flesh!

[8] We cannot give details of the unlimited literature that v. 16b has produced. In most cases the main target has been the declaration about the knowledge of Christ. But this is really an adjunct, which justifies and confirms the *major* assertion that we no longer know anyone after the flesh. The case of Christ is at once the extreme and the original case, the one that determines the knowledge of every individual and every thing. For a good interpretation of this passage, cf. J. B. Soucek, 'Wir kennen Christus nicht mehr nach dem Fleisch', *EvTh* 19, 1959, pp. 300–21. But we think that we must not confine this new knowledge to the members of the Body of Christ, as he tends to do.

[9] See p. 33 above, and particularly *En Christ*, pp. 45ff.

[10] *ETR*, 1959, pp. 131–2.

Life in Christ and a New Creation

ways,[11] but, whatever method is preferred, our attention is drawn to the appearance of the *new creature*. He is new for two reasons. On the one hand, he has come into being quite recently, from the act of redemption that has just taken place (see the 'now' of v. 16) —a new situation is created.[12] On the other hand, he is new because he already depends on the world to come; to him alone its advent in history bears witness of the eschatological significance of the three days that shook the world; and its first steps crack the foundations of the age that is passing; a new genesis is coming into being, a future that has already begun.

Thus the present reality of life in Christ cannot overlap that of the new creation that is still to come. What we have just seen of the new creature, however, shows that the two are not without connection, which we shall seek to clarify through reference to other texts; these, although they are naturally not the best known, are no less significant on that account.

We see this in Col. 2.17, which would be translated literally, 'Therefore let no one pass judgment on you in questions of food and drink or with regard to a festival or a new moon or a sabbath (v. 16). These are only a shadow of what is to come; but the body of Christ . . .' The general meaning is comparatively clear: the various observances 'testified to an aspiration for spiritual good things which, before Christ came, were inaccessible. In the pre-Christian world they were on certain points the unsubstantial shadow and yet the harbinger of a Body belonging to Christ. For it is in Christ alone that the good things to come—forgiveness, sanctification, communion with God, life—are present and accessible to believers, in his *Body* which is the Church.'[13] Yet, when it is examined closely, Paul's phraseology is elliptical to the

---

[11] P. H. Menoud and J. Héring use the Vulgate's punctuation: 'For one who is a new creature in Christ, the old world has passed away, and behold, it has been made anew.' But the suppression of clear-cut division blurs the progress of the thought, and seems to us to reduce what the apostle said to a bald statement of fact. The traditional punctuation, on the other hand, emphasizes the stages of the argument—if anyone is in Christ, he is a new creature; consequently, the old course of things is superseded, there is something new.

[12] Everything that went before the cross and the resurrection is marked by old age, either because it came from the world 'after the flesh' (e.g. 'the old man'), or because it belonged to a previous dispensation ('the old covenant', II Cor. 3.14; 'the old written code', Rom. 7.6).

[13] Masson, CNT I, *ad loc*.

point of resembling an enigma that has been given many different answers.[14] It seems, as the Jerusalem Bible suggests, that Paul uses the word 'body' ambiguously.[15] It is introduced as opposed to 'shadow' through the contrast *skia—sōma* used by other writers such as Philo and Josephus;[16] and so it implies, in relation to the fleeting and evanescent form of the shadow, the idea of solid reality. But hardly is the word written when Paul slips straight into the expression 'the Body of Christ', which he already had in mind —is it not *in Christo* that the good things of the world to come are already actually present?[17] So we can legitimately translate 'but the reality is the Body of Christ', and thus feel the full force of the text.

We may also look at I Cor. 5.6–8; here again the Body of Christ appears as the new reality and herald. The church in Corinth is involved in and defiled by a scandal of a sexual nature. The apostle urges the Church, as it is already purified, to expel all impurity, and, as it is already unleavened,[18] to expel all old leaven. He makes a comparison that is explained only by the Jewish custom of the Passover. We know that every trace of leaven had to disappear from all Israelite homes before the first day of the feast. Dough, mixed with yeast, is a symbol of what is perishable and corruptible[19]—of the old world—whereas unleavened bread is regarded as the new reality of the eschatological feast. The latter may be celebrated, since Christ, the paschal lamb, has been sacrificed. The exhortation not to let oneself be contaminated by what is left of the old life is based on the Lord's Supper, the feast of the new bread. By it the Church's members become a single Body to form

---

[14] Compare with John 13.34: 'A *new* commandment I give to you . . .' The ancient commandment of love is new because henceforth the imperative follows from what Christ has just accomplished ('As I have loved you . . .'). Cf. O. Cullmann, *Christ and Time*, pp. 224ff. See Masson, p. 131 n. 1. We think with him that the reference to the Church, to which attention is rarely drawn, is undeniable.

[15] P. Benoit, *ad loc.*

[16] M. Dibelius, HNT 12, *ad loc.*

[17] P. Benoit's accurate intuition is expressed in equivocal terms when he writes in the explanatory note, 'The physical body of the risen Christ which is the essential eschatological reality, the germ of the new universe.' We shall see how far we can speak of *germ*, but in any case one could not use the word about 'the physical body of the risen Christ'!

[18] Paul's dialectic is here, as always, vigorous and forceful. It is well brought out here, in connection with this passage, by W. G. Kümmel in the supplement to Lietzmann, HNT 9.

[19] H. Windisch, art. ζύμη, *TWNT* II, pp. 906 and 907, quotes examples in which 'leaven' becomes synonymous with 'liable to putrefaction'.

Life in Christ and a New Creation

these unleavened loaves, purified by the redemptive sacrifice.[20] The presence and life of the Christian community mean that from now onwards the celebration of the Passover of the last days has begun.

It is as well to recall the idea of *inheritance*, so firmly joined to that of the Kingdom of God that it introduces the term most frequently in the epistles (I Cor. 6.9, 10; Gal. 5.21; cf. Eph. 5.5). Belonging to Christ, who is the only offspring of Abraham (Gal. 3.16), the Church is Abraham's authentic posterity, and therefore the Body of the heirs according to promise (Gal. 3.29). That Body is henceforth open to all nations: such is the mystery of Christ according to Eph. 3.6. Even if the inheritance is in the future, believers are henceforth 'qualified . . . to share in the inheritance of the saints in light';[21] more still, they have received its pledge and guarantee in the gift of the *pneuma* (II Cor. 1.22; 5.5).[22]

There is an analogous idea in the passages that mention 'first-fruits'. But the emphasis has shifted: the 'earnest' concerns the final recovery of salvation, announced and promised to those who have received the 'earnest', whereas the first-fruits are put into a universal context, being concerned not only with the whole of redemption but with all the redeemed.[23] In I Cor. 15.20–23 it is Christ, the risen Man, who appears as the advance guard, signifying for all who are his their share in the same resurrection, in such

---

[20] Cf. J. Héring, *CNT* VII, *ad loc*. But the reference to the eucharist is not, as Héring suggests, superadded to the exhortation ('besides the exhortation . . .'); it forms the basis of it, just as in the other passages of the epistle (see H. von Soden, *Sakrament und Ethik bei Paulus*).

[21] C. Masson rightly distinguishes with Foerster (*TWNT* III, art. κλῆρος and κληρονόμος) between 'inheritance' and 'portion' which appears here in Col. 1.12 [AV and RSV: 'inheritance']. The 'portion' recalls that Canaan (or the Kingdom) falls to the share of the believer by the grace of God. 'The inheritance expresses the duration and legitimacy of the possession' that is derived from it. Just as the portion assured to everyone his share of the common inheritance in Canaan, so it is with regard to the Kingdom.

[22] The expression 'earnest of the Spirit' (as in AV) must not cause confusion; we have received not merely a first instalment of the Spirit (as if the *pneuma* could be granted in part!), but the Spirit itself as an instalment of final redemption.

[23] 'First-fruits' may also mean believers—Epenetus, the first-fruits of Asia for Christ (Rom. 16.5); Stephanas and his household, whom Paul himself had baptized at Corinth, the first-fruits of Achaia (I Cor. 16.15). Strictly speaking, the meaning here is not eschatological; the expressions are to be understood in the light of the apostle's missionary ministry (Rom. 15.16), the sacrificial offering of the continents —Asia, Achaia—to the Lord; Epenetus or Stephanas are not only the first sign of this, but even now the reality. In their persons—*pars pro toto*—the Gentile nations are consecrated and offered to Christ. Cf. A. Butte, *Les offrandes sacrificielles du chrétien dans le Nouveau Testament*, typewritten thesis, Montpellier, 1959.

Christianity According to Paul

solidarity that their non-resurrection would nullify that of Christ himself (I Cor. 15.16). But we must pay special attention to Romans 8: the first-fruits are the Spirit. Through its outpouring, the final transformation of our entire person into a 'spiritual' being is as if already given and made present, although it is still awaited (v. 23). In this fundamental development we see the concepts of first-fruits and inheritance unite. Both stem from our new condition in Christ: we have received the spirit of adoption. Now we are sons of God, and we can approach the Father with the cry, 'Abba!' 'And if children, then [we are] heirs, heirs of God and fellow heirs with Christ . . .' (v. 17). This adoption also means our glorious liberation, whose repercussions shake all creation. Dragged into slavery by man, it pants and sighs for deliverance. For the world, too, these first glimmerings of the freedom that is found anew in Christ are as the dawn of the day of glory. The new man, re-established in the image of God, rediscovers his original destiny, and now appears at last as the one whom the universe awaits in order to attain its end.[24] The Church is the sign that foretells the glorious recovery, like the embryo that creation carries within itself, already in the pangs of travail.

Such, then, is the aim of the *election* of the Church, which is called to form the people renewed in the Son's image, so that the Son may not appear alone, but as the first-born among many brethren (v. 29), the first-born of every creature (Col. 1.15, AV), the first-born from the dead (Col. 1.18); he is likewise the first-born of the new creation, the beginning of the race of those whom God has consecrated to himself by choosing them out of all the nations of the earth.[25] Thus there is nothing restrictive to mark the choice of those whom God has called, justified, and glorified; like the election of Abraham, the election of the Church has in view the blessing of all nations. The Body of Christ is built up so as to become, for the world and for all creation, the very hope of the Kingdom.

---

[24] Cf. F. J. Leenhardt, CNT VI, *ad loc.*
[25] Cf. A. Butte, *op. cit.*, ch. IV. ' "Israel is my first-born son" (Ex. 4.22). The idea of sacrifice is in the foreground. "I consecrate him to myself" says the Lord. This is the basis of Israel's priestly function. Chosen above the nations, Israel is sacrificed and consecrated for the nations. And in the midst of Israel, chosen above the twelve tribes, Levi is chosen instead of and in the place of all the first-born of Israel' (Num. 3.12; 4.1, 2; 8.18).

Life in Christ and a New Creation

Thus we see taking shape the Church's scope and also its relativity: the Kingdom is its end in both meanings of the word—the Kingdom, and through it the world, too. In Christ it is, like the believer himself, in the position of a servant. A mission has been entrusted to it, which is its *raison d'être* here below, and which uses it in the service at once of the *leitourgia* towards God, and of the *diakonia* and the ministry of the Word towards the world.

We must be clear about this subordination of the Church. We get a striking indication of it by bringing together two texts, viz. I Cor. 15.28 (AV), 'When all things are subjected to him, then the Son himself will also be subjected to him who put all things under him, that *God may be all in all*', and Col. 3.11, 'Here there cannot be Greek and Jew, circumcised and uncircumcised, barbarian, Scythian, slave, free man, but *Christ is all, and in all.*' Paul's words are not to suggest any pantheism in heaven, or any 'pan-Christ-ism' on earth. The development of I Corinthians 15 shows clearly enough that the apostle does not think of the final resurrection as being achieved in the reabsorption of all the 'glorious bodies' in the divinity. We must, with J. Héring, regard it as meaning 'so that God may be totally present in the universe'. In the same way, as we have already emphasized, Col. 3.11 does not imagine the Church as a society where personalities have been absorbed in Christ's; but Christ assures to everyone in it a fulness of life and the fulfilment of his calling.[26] We find a striking analogy here between the Kingdom and the Church that foreshadows it: God's total sovereignty in the future world is matched by Christ's total sovereignty in his Body. And just as 'men will come from east and west, and from north and south, and sit at table in the kingdom of God' (Luke 13.29) to show the fulness of the Father's mercy, so there are to gather together in the Christian community Greek and Jew, barbarian and Scythian, slave and free man, so that it may consist of a true image of universal reconciliation, and every kind of opposition may be grasped and overcome in Christ.

But when we bring these two texts together we see the Church's particularism, which is the particularism of election. A similar mysterious boundary separates the Father's reign from the Son's, and the Church from the new creation. God is the ruler (the head)

---

[26] Cf. Eph. 1.23. The Church is called the *plērōma* of Christ 'not because it completes him, but because Christ is completely active in it' (P. Bonnard).

of Christ (I Cor. 11.3), as Christ is the ruler, and the head, of the Body. The living Christ lives for God (Rom. 6.10)—and 'if we live, we live to the Lord [Christ]' (Rom. 14.8). 'All are yours; and you are Christ's; and Christ is God's' (I Cor. 3.22, 23). We may indeed say that Christ's body is the seed of the new creation, and yet we can admit no continuous development from one to the other. We have already seen that Paul does not take for granted that his self will be progressively transformed; he awaits unwaveringly his final redemption at the time of the Lord's parousia. Nor is there any slow process of maturing that would one day bring the Church to the dimensions of the Kingdom that is to come; nothing but Christ's advent in glory will unlock the passage from one to the other, 'when he delivers the kingdom to God the Father'. The Church will not become the Kingdom any more than the Son will take the place of the Father. No doubt the growth of the Body is mentioned more than once.[27] But this growth takes place more in height than in extent, 'up . . . into . . . the head' —it is a question of attaining 'to the measure of the stature of the fulness of Christ', of growing 'into a holy temple in the Lord'. Nowhere does the apostle allow us to catch sight of a growth in majesty, to which every age would bring its contribution, and which would enable the Church to coincide with the whole of humanity. It is certainly necessary for the gospel to reach the ends of the earth, but that is for the gathering in of Scythian and barbarian, the slave and the free man in Christ. The Church's full dimension is that which is assigned to it by the mysterious boundaries of its election. Its calling is to be an embassy of the reconciliation that has been carried out, and to give the world the perfect image of Christ, that is to say the union in one and the same Body of those whom everything had hitherto separated. The Church is no more co-extensive with the universe than Israel's mission was to assimilate the nations of the world; the Church, elected like Israel for the blessing of the world, as long as history lasts, remains 'the community of the dispersion', and its faithfulness urges it on continually to become more and more explicitly the emblem of its Lord. The particularism of election in no way lessens Jesus Christ's sovereign claim on the whole of mankind;

[27] Cf. Col. 2.19; Eph. 4.16; see Eph. 2.21. We have noted that the only *progress* was that of the gospel in the world (Phil. 1.5; Col. 1.6); cf. above.

Life in Christ and a New Creation

on the contrary, from the very composition of the Church, it intimates and asserts it.

Probably more than one reader has been wanting for some time to interrupt and reproach us with not having done justice to the captivity epistles;[28] we have quoted certain verses as if by the way; but it is difficult to make a detour that will not seem too long.

We have recalled, in their essentials, the anxieties that Paul's correspondents caused him or his disciple when the letters were written, and we have sketched the kind of change of thought that they involve on more grounds than one. If we have met this on the plane of personal relationships, it is not surprising to see it return here on the plane of the Church. The change has already concerned the expression *in Christo* itself; as we followed its evolution, we saw the transfer from the ecclesiological to the theological sense, as if the construction were being transposed, God substituting himself for man, considered as the subject of the sentence; the words thereupon acquired a universal application, which could be widened so far as to embrace the whole of the divine plan.[29] But the concepts of 'the Church' and 'the Body of Christ' have also been changed, considerably enough to have impressed the exegetes, who, according to their own particular outlook, have given the changes more or less weight. The Church, though primarily concerned with the solid local reality of a present messianic community, also receives a dimension that is universal in space and eternal in time, to become the one and only Church, a reality in itself and independent of those who compose it. The evolution of the concept of the Body of Christ is analogous. First, it means a Body in Christ, the emphasis being on the union of different members;[30] in the two epistles that we have in mind here it receives the definite article and becomes a quasi-personified reality, of cosmopolitan extent and capable of growth, but with the members left in the background; this Body now appears as more distinct from Christ himself, as is shown by the development

---

[28] At any rate those that are disputed, Colossians and Ephesians.

[29] *En Christ*, ch. V, par. 3. Examples: '*In Christo* we live a new life' becomes '*In Christo* God has gathered all together.'

[30] Some will see its origin in the social body beloved of the Stoics; others, like O. Cullmann, in Paul's sacramental realism.

of the concept Christ as the head, directing and inspiring the whole organism.[31]

The exegetes' reactions are obviously very varied. For some, such as C. Masson, we have left the Pauline horizon, since, as we have noticed, temporal eschatology has been succeeded by a kind of spatial eschatology in which the body grows till it has achieved its full stature.[32] Others, such as E. Percy, try to harmonize the *homologoumena* and the *antilegomena*, finding in them all the characteristics of a genuinely Pauline inspiration—but, we must admit, the demonstration is rather rapid![33] H. Schlier has devoted his life to these epistles and, in the commentary on Ephesians which is the outcome of his researches, he gives up scarcely any of the views which caused such a stir in his youth, but his interests as a comparative student of religions have been succeeded by those of the theologian. There is no doubt that in his view, in the letter to the Ephesians, the Church pre-exists all creation and, *a fortiori*, all those who compose it. It is identical with 'the new aeon', 'the heavenly city', 'the eternal praise of God which God has acquired for himself'.[34] Schlier tries, not to place side by side, but to unite, this hypostatized concept of the Body of Christ with the community concept—these two aspects are intimately bound up together, since the Body of Christ is at one and the same time 'the *cosmos* embracing everything' and a form to be restricted by boundaries, a form transcending every human being and a *communio sanctorum*. This would explain the Church's nature, which is sacramental and institutional (arising from this cosmic dimension) as well as charismatic and existential (because of its social dimension). An excellent study of P. Benoit seems to us to have the great merit

[31] As is also shown in the fine development of Eph. 5, in which the mystery of the Church is grasped in the conjugal relation of husband and wife.

[32] Cf. *Ephésiens* (CNT IX), p. 199.

[33] E. Percy, *Der Leib Christi*. The basic thesis is that of the incorporation of believers in Jesus Christ himself as a historical person who died on the cross and was raised again according to the Spirit. The only thing that changes from one epistle to another is the point of view. The underlying fact remains the same, and on it the apostle Paul stands firm—believers form *one* Body in Christ, and Christ is the Lord and the life-source of that unique Body. Percy, a valiant anti-Gnostic, fights on all fronts (this, as well as that of the Fourth Gospel) against those who like to explain the origins of Christian literature in the light of gnosis—in this case Schlier, elsewhere Bultmann or Käsemann.

[34] *Der Brief an die Epheser*, Düsseldorf, 2nd ed., 1958. Compare with the study on 'L'Eglise d'après l'épître aux Ephésiens' included in the *Temps de l'Eglise*, Tournai, 1961. The quotations are taken especially from two excursuses in the commentary, one on the *sōma*, and the other on the *plērōma* (pp. 90ff.).

Life in Christ and a New Creation

of elucidating convincingly at least two important points: (1) The development of the role attributed to the Head does not arise from speculation about the Body, but takes up the old biblical expression so as to indicate Christ's universal supremacy, extended over principalities and powers; it was applied to the Body only secondarily, and thence changed into the Hellenizing meaning of vital nutritive principle, animating the organism. (2) The introduction of the concept *plērōma*. 'The apostle', writes Benoit, 'always regards the Body of Christ as limited to the group of saved men constituting the Church; to indicate the extension of Christ's work he uses another term—*plērōma*'; no speculation justifies its presence: it is a question of keeping the specific value of the *sōma* and at the same time 'integrating into the new world *in Christo* the heavenly powers and the material world that they rule . . .'[35]

For the rest, the author admits an analogous concept in his broad outline of the Body of Christ according to Paul; it is formulated from the first epistles onwards, starting from the eucharistic experience.

The reader will not expect us to interfere in so weighty a discussion; but he will already have noted some assertions that may run counter to the conclusions that we have just reached. It is unreasonable to expect an exegesis to harmonize everything. These two epistles, just as they are and whoever wrote them, seem to us valuable on more than one ground, taken with the Pauline texts as a whole.

1. By extolling the unity of the divine work, which is completely summed up in Christ, and by starting from him to go on towards creation and the final completion, these epistles erected a rampart against the attractions of the mystery religions, into which there was always the danger that Christianity would let itself be dragged. The Church would then have been nothing more than an institution for ensuring immortality.[36]

2. Christ's sovereignty over his Body is not the beginning of his sovereignty over the world—it is the result of it. This perspective is fundamental if we are to grasp the relationship between

---
[35] 'Corps, tête et plérôme dans les épîtres de la captivité', art. of 1956, published in *Exégèse et théologie* II, Paris, 1961, pp. 107ff. The expressions about the 'new world' are ambiguous (see above).

[36] See O. Cullmann, *The Earliest Christian Confessions*, ET, 1949. On the deviations of Ignatius, according to whom creation is already passing into eclipse, see T. Preiss, *La vie en Christ*.

the Church and the world. By inverting the terms we justify all Caesaro-papist imperialisms; by preserving them we define the Church's mission, break down the barriers between it and the world, put aside the constant insidious temptations to reconstitute within it a para-creation, having its own institutions, life, and *milieu*—Christ's sovereignty is not bicephalous![37]

3. On a similar plane to that of the 'life hidden with Christ in God', these epistles remind us that the reality of the Church is no more at our command than is our own Christian life. And if the Church can always be seen in the community through the power of the Holy Spirit, it, too, has that mysterious and royal face which escapes us, lit up by the light of Christ and sharing in his ministry at the right hand of the Father, not yet in the reign, but in the adoration, the praise, and the communion of the blessed, and in the struggle against principalities and powers. Just as we are not without him on earth, so he is not without us in heaven.

But there our assertions have to stop abruptly. And we must emphasize at once the dangers of an ecclesiology that is based only on the captivity epistles, or that gives them too exclusive an importance. We have already noted a few examples of this in passages quoted above: the Church becomes that universal, eternal entity[38] that inevitably merges in the Kingdom. Perhaps in the degree that we recognize the eucharistic origin of the concept 'Church, Body of Christ', we thereby recognize its boundaries, which are exactly the same as those of the sacrament. 'It is clear that in his letters to the Colossians and the Ephesians St

---

[37] We may recall O. Cullmann's classical study on 'The Kingship of Christ and the Church in the New Testament', ET in *The Early Church*, 1956.

[38] We have been glad to see an orthodox theologian take a strong stand against the concept of a universal Church, a concept of Latin origin, inspired as much by Stoicism as the *imperium romanum*, and of which 'we should never have found the idea in the New Testament, particularly in St Paul's writings, if that idea had not already been in our minds'! He recognizes only one ecclesiology that is faithful to Paul's teaching—the one that he calls *eucharistic*: 'The local church is the Body of Christ in its eucharistic aspect. . . . Every local church is the Church of God in Christ, for Christ is in his Body in the eucharistic assembly, and it is thanks to communion with the Body of Christ that the faithful become members of his Body. . . . Every local church shows all the fulness of the Church of God, for it is the Church of God and not simply one part of it.

'Eucharistic ecclesiology, then, does not at all reject the Church's universality, but it distinguishes between external universality, considered as the limits of its mission, and internal universality, which always and in all circumstances simply means itself, for it means that the Church manifests itself everywhere and always in its fulness and unity.' N. Afanassieff, *La Primauté de Pierre*, Neuchâtel, 1960, pp. 26ff.

Life in Christ and a New Creation

Paul makes the Church, the Body of Christ, in some way coextensive with the *cosmos*, the whole integrated universe . . . a heavenly and eternal existence, in relation both to Christ who is its head and to the elect of whom it is composed.' These words from P. Benoit, which it is not easy to reconcile with those quoted above ('The Body of Christ always remains limited to the group of saved men constituting the Church') are preceded by this assertion, which seems to be the very opposite of the conclusions that we had reached: 'On the contrary, Scripture asks us to widen the Church's territory so that it shall include all the saved, whoever they are, and to lengthen its duration so far as to include eternity.'[39]

So now we are warned once more of the danger of trying to build an ecclesiology on only one of the many aspects that Pauline literature presents. This is particularly true of the idea of the 'Body of Christ', which runs all the more risk of deviations as it is not directly joined to any Old Testament theme.[40] Any interpretation of it must always be corrected and explained by the reality that we find at the heart of Scripture—that of God's people and the messianic community.[41]

The Body of Christ, then, the figure-head of the new creation, does not merge in the world that follows in its wake. It contains everything *in nuce*, beginning with the first-fruits of the Spirit and the strength of *agapē*, so that people have talked of a germ—very well, *sed Pauli modo, non physicorum*. The final resurrection of the body, as it is presented in I Cor. 15 with the help of an analogy, did not involve the slow ripening of the seed, but its sudden blossoming in glory, in which the laws of nature stand aside to yield pride of place to the supreme intervention of the Lord, the Creator.

2. NEWNESS OF LIFE

What we have just written could not in the very least devalue the role now assigned to the Body of Christ—quite the contrary.

---

[39] 'Le baptême des enfants et la doctrine biblique du Baptême selon O. Cullmann', *Exégèse et théologie* II, p. 222.
[40] See *En Christ*, ch. IV, par. 2. The Old Testament roots are to be sought in the idea of corporate personality.
[41] The lasting value both of K. L. Schmidt's article ἐκκλησία, in *TWNT* III, 502ff. (ET, *The Church* [Bible Key Words 2], 1950), and of L. Cerfaux's *The Church in the Theology of St Paul*, is that they have brought this aspect fully to light.

Christianity According to Paul

Before the eternal day when God will be all in all, Christ is today all in all in the Christian community, however humble it may be. The study of the Gospels has shown the intimate connection between saying and being, between Christ's words and his person; the study of the epistles reveals in the Church the authentic sign, the parable that necessarily accompanies the preaching of the Kingdom. It is the first fruits of the Word, and its joint incarnation. So with the same enthusiasm with which he preaches the gospel, Paul builds up the churches; the two tasks are one, and in them he is a worker with Christ, the Lord of the Word and the Life of the Body.

This appears to be of decisive importance for understanding the unity of Paul's work and the cohesion of his thought; no dividing line appears between the missionary and the pastoral ministries, just as there is no frontier marking out ecclesiology from ethics; we are not now at two sources, but at the only source that he will allow 'of morals and religion'.[42] It is no use looking there, as too many have tried to do, for the slightest moral, social, or religious principle. All is realism; there is no question of laying down the ideas and leading lines of a new religion or of initiating a system: every decision flows from the acquired and verified knowledge of the presence of the Body of Christ. That is the great eschatological *fact*; a new reality has appeared in this world, a gift of God, a creation of the Spirit, beginning with baptism and the Lord's Supper. That is the point from which everything originates and proceeds; coming from what has been, and going on to meet what is to come, ethics are bound up with the most intimate aspect of life in Christ; they cannot be dissociated from the life of the community; both are bearers of the Word and both are missionary by nature.

Probably the most striking examples can be taken from I Corinthians. A young church is at grips with the thousand problems and dangers caused by the intrusion of a new body into an old world. To belong elsewhere, must one deliberately cut the ties that still bind Christians to all their surroundings—beginning with their own flesh and blood? How is this new reality to be written into the heart of life's relationships? There are so many questions coming in from all directions and already getting the most varied

[42] Cf. Pascal: 'Doctrine and morality. It is all the body of Jesus Christ.'

Life in Christ and a New Creation

and even contradictory answers from within the community. For some it will be asceticism; for others, 'all things are lawful'; for everyone, already, a temptation to a complete break which, moreover, is being shown in their own divisions. Everyone is eager to get back to the familiar ways of religiosity or human morals. But against this many-faced dualism and the dissension that it brings, Paul stands firm with his single answer. We can hardly see any logical arrangements in this letter; everything comes in—personal news, apostolic ministry, local problems of a growing congregation; everything is intermingled—factions in the church, lawsuits, women's behaviour, conduct when invited out, purchases at the butcher's, love-feasts with the brethren, finances, the Lord's Supper, one who is behaving scandalously, marriage, and suddenly the immense horizon of the coming of the Kingdom. What diversity—the impact of the gospel, and of the world, on all levels. And yet what unity. Never, perhaps, has theology done its work better, illuminating everything in Christ—that is to say, bringing it to the light of his cross, his return, and his presence. You might think you were faced with a minor question, a merely incidental matter, and now you see that everything is at stake. The misleading distinctions made by our idealist churches between so-called spiritual and material problems simply do not exist. No law, no ordinance, still less any casuistry; every question derives from the same central reality that Paul is continually bringing back to hold before the eyes of his converts—their forgiveness, their justification, their belonging to Christ, and their life in him. Whatever the question at issue, he resolves it by appealing to the Body of Christ as to the supreme, indisputable fact. The building up of the Church and personal morality come to one and the same thing, converging in the manifestation of the life in Christ which is the glory of God. To bring that life into prominence, to give it expression, body, and shape, to keep it humble and royal, absolutely spiritual, resolutely practical, and genuinely Corinthian—that is what the apostle is striving for, with every member from the least to the greatest, and every problem, too, playing a part. Paul's journeys, the discussions with the Corinthians, and the questions connected with them—these are what stand out at first sight. But the cloud is rent, and behind it there appears, dominating the scene, the great drama of redemption and the outline of the Kingdom.

This ethic, fundamentally one in its inspiration, is remarkably varied in its motivation, which, in different ways, is at last perforce linked with Christology. Thus, in I Corinthians we can always hear overtones of what is to become the classic distinction between the three offices, the note being sometimes priestly, sometimes kingly, and sometimes prophetic. We offer the following examples.

In chapter 3.16–20 God's temple is mentioned for the first time: 'Do you not know . . .?' This reproof appears whenever Paul has to come back to the essentials of what he has taught his converts. Some people have thought that this passage is out of place in this context;[43] on the contrary, it seems to take up and summarize all the themes that form the beginning of the letter. It is a question of the discord that is being stirred up by the claim of certain members of the church at Corinth to true wisdom. Faced with these disputes, Paul goes back to the source. We know the importance of the temple of God in the New Testament[44]—it is a theme closely joined to that of the Body of Christ, to which he returns continually. The rites of purification and the sacrifices of atonement are fulfilled in that of the cross; and in the same way the temple of Jerusalem is replaced by the person of Jesus. In him the Church, which is Christ's Body, appears as the spiritual dwelling-place of the end of time, proclaimed by the prophets and connecting the sanctuary of the old covenant, built and demolished by turns, with the heavenly and eternal sanctuary where God's presence will enlighten the new creation. The privileges attached to the Jerusalem temple have been transferred to the Body of Christ: at Corinth God lives in this Church which belongs to him body and soul, where his love is in action, his holiness and his glory dwell. Innumerable ritual ordinances surrounded the cultic practices and put fences about God's holy presence among a rebellious people. Any infringement was blasphemous, and was felt to deserve death. Henceforth the blasphemy is not the illegal crossing into the sacred princincts, but the offering of any affront to the Body, whether individually—we shall come back to this— or collectively: by its divisions the church of Corinth is committ-

---

[43] Cf. J. Héring, CNT VII, *ad loc*.
[44] In all the groups of writings, Pauline, synoptic, Johannine, I Peter, etc. See, e.g., O. Cullmann, *Les sacrements dans l'Evangile johannique*, Paris, 1951, pp. 41ff.

Life in Christ and a New Creation

ing sacrilege, for the cultic ceremonies have been succeeded, for the glory of God, by the building up of the Church. By claiming to belong to Peter, or Paul, or Apollos, or 'to Christ', the Corinthians are destroying God's work; they are stretching a guilty hand over the sacred place and signing their own death-warrant, just as everyone who approached Mount Sinai was stoned to death. An affront to the Church is an affront to God; to break the unity of the Body is to profane his holiness.

The same line of thought inspires the apostle's attitude towards unchastity. To condemn any liaison with a prostitute (6.12ff.) he makes no appeal to divine law or to the great principles of human morality. His reaction is remarkable—any such relation is forbidden because it represents an outrage on the Body of Christ! In the sexual union the two partners become one flesh, and likewise we, when we are united to Christ, form one single Body in him.[45] Within that Body the only possible sexual relation is that of husband and wife, which is given its full meaning and allows them to 'glorify God in [their bodies]'. But a union outside marriage profanes that prior union with Christ which the apostle considers to be, for our body, real and as momentous as the physical union. Belonging to Christ and belonging to a prostitute are incompatible. Every other sin that a man commits is outside his own body. Morally and spiritually, perhaps, there are more serious faults, but this sin takes on a religious character, that of profaning the temple dedicated to God.[46]

At the beginning of the same chapter (6) we are told of a lawsuit between two church members. The news makes the apostle indignant. A dispute between two brethren which is serious enough to start a lawsuit is certainly a fault (v. 7); what is inadmissible is to have taken the case to a Gentile court. Not that Paul contests in

---

[45] Literally 'a same spirit'. But in the Pauline perspective the two expressions meet here. Cf. E. Percy, *Der Leib Christi*, p. 11.

[46] This remains true, even if we do not discover, with J. Héring, behind the prostitute the figure of the goddess of carnal love (CNT VII, p. 48).

On the other hand, Paul declares to the spouse who is worried at not having been able to convert an unbelieving husband or wife that his or her own sharing in the Body of Christ sanctifies the partner; the latter also belongs to the Body of Christ through the former, since together they are one flesh. Without ceasing to pray, the believer is to apply himself, not to putting pressure on what does not depend on him (the other's conversion), but to watching over what does depend on him and will at last redound the more surely to the other's good—his own sanctification. That is what matters.

itself the validity of the State, or the office of magistrate; he does not doubt that the Roman State has actually received from God the mission of maintaining peace and justice in the Mediterranean region. His indignation and insistence reflect the importance that he attaches to the Church's situation in the world. We know that the Jewish communities within the Empire had had the benefit of a statute that conferred on them, with a right to the jurisdiction of their own courts, a kind of extra-territorial privilege.[47] That was, as it were, a sign of the special nature of God's people called to live in the world without being subject to it, and, like the ambassador of a foreign power, to be answerable to another sovereign, even in the country where they are living. Paul urgently wants the Christian community to inherit this tradition, and to carry within itself the visible and indisputable signs of being under a new jurisdiction—the Church is henceforth under the law of the Kingdom, of which it is the advance-guard. By initiating a lawsuit against one another the church members are breaking up their new relationship in Christ; they are going back to the former situation in which this court was one whose rulings they recognized, just as the Galatians were putting themselves back under the yoke of the law, or as the Colossians were going back to the elements and principles of this world. In seeking to have their affairs settled by an authority external to Christ, they are denying that they belong in common to him. And now there comes the *prophetic* thought—the saints will judge the world! Does not this eschatological mission qualify them, from now on, to judge the less important matters? The Church's hope is mocked when its members' behaviour in effect repudiates their glorious destiny.

Finally, the apostle has to tackle the persistent problem of what the believer may and may not do. Here it is a question connected with food, and it is referred to in I Corinthians 8 and in Romans 14. Is it right to buy at the butcher's, and to eat at home, food already offered to idols? Some saw no harm in doing so. Others were afraid of coming into contact with the demons to whom the food had been offered. There were the same doubts, too, when one was invited to a meal with a Gentile: what attitude was to be taken? The 'strong' say that it is a matter of no importance, since idols do not exist. The 'weak' are uneasy in their conscience, and some-

[47] Cf. Lietzmann, HNT 9, *ad loc.*

Life in Christ and a New Creation

times allow themselves to be led into actions of which at heart they disapprove ('Whatever does not proceed from faith is sin', Rom. 14.23). The question is referred to the apostle. The 'strong' are counting on his unqualified approval. Really, Paul replies, you are still at the elementary stage, since you are arguing about this matter. It is quite true that idols do not exist; we have only one God from whom everything comes, and only one Lord, through whom everything exists. True, you have been set free by Christ; you belong to Christ the Lord; everything is yours, past, present, and future, life and death; all things are lawful, and to the pure all things are pure. A royal freedom opens out before anyone who is subject to the King, and it is no longer open to question. Yet this freedom carries in itself the original danger of the fall, namely that man may use it to set himself free of the Lord and go his own way: 'Take care lest this liberty . . . become a stumbling-block . . .' is the apostle's great anxiety. If, therefore, it inspires every decision, it must be within a certain ordering—that which conforms to the laws of the life of Christ's Body. The Lord's *kingship*, the source of royal freedom, is expressed in that of one's brother: it is to the latter that attitudes and decisions must be related and subordinated. 'All of you be subject one to another' (I Peter 5.5, AV). That certainly does not destroy this freedom, but ensures its specific quality—it dies when it affronts one's brother, weakens a member who is already weak, or leads astray a neighbour who is liable to fall; when you sin thus against a brother, when you wound his tender conscience, you sin against Christ himself and wound his Body!

The sovereign way that is open in Christ, the 'more excellent way', must be the way of love. We again find here the tracks of Christian freedom of which we spoke above, where the royalty of God's children is shown in their complete willingness to serve their neighbour: 'By faith, the Christian is master of all, by love he is servant of all'; this remark by Luther, which we have already quoted, takes us, more than any other, to the heart of Pauline morality.

Thus the apostle's ethic is dominated by a striking view of the newness of the gospel. The most complete of revolutions is going to be realized without any revolution, Christianity accepting all,

Christianity According to Paul

except sin, to achieve all. It would have been tempting to declaim about the wickedness and immorality of the surrounding world, about the tensions created even within the Church itself between the circumcised and the uncircumcised, the coming of the 'great day', and the complete and abrupt break with the past. But that would have meant permanently debilitating the unique virtue of the Christian faith and merging it inescapably in idealist, reformist, or revolutionary movements (they all join) which break, wave by wave, on the shores of the centuries. That does not mean that Christianity is going to tolerate everything, or 'baptize' everything; it means that its revolution cannot merge in any other. The future world is not its aim, but as it were its origin, in proportion as it is coming, or is already present, in Christ. To the various points of view that sought to attract the newly converted Corinthians, Paul replies simply and unequivocally, 'Every one should remain in the state in which he was called.' This exhortation is addressed, in the ebb and flow of I Corinthians 7, to married (1–6, 10–12) and unmarried Christians (8, 9), to those who are separated (11), to married couples of whom only one is a believer (12, 16), to the circumcised and the uncircumcised (18, 19), to slaves (21–23), to the unmarried (25–28), to engaged people vowed to continence (36–38), to widows (39, 40).[48] It is from within, through the work of Christ, who is all and in all in every one of these conditions, and not through levelling down or squaring up, that all things are made new, and that one day, much more certainly, slavery will perish and the status of women be completely transformed. Freedom comes through the incorporation of everyone in Christ, with his human condition intact; it is achieved through the living strength of the Spirit, the effective action of the Lord's Supper, the virtue of love, acting in harmony within the communion of the brethren. Whether we are on the theological plane (relations between circumcised and uncircumcised), or the social (relations between slaves and free men), or the conjugal (relations between husband and wife, or the position of the betrothed and of the single person), Paul's attitude is distinguished by its coherence. In Christ the man or wife, and the betrothed, the Gentile uncircumcised through his calling, the Jew circumcised through the realization of the promise, the slave, free

---

[48] See J. J. von Allmen, *Maris et femmes d'après saint Paul*, p. 11.

Life in Christ and a New Creation

in the Lord, and his master, the Lord's slave, all have found their human destiny.

3. RECAPITULATION

At the end of a work that has never left us unmoved, Albert Schweitzer, on taking leave of Pauline mysticism, considers that, notwithstanding its inspiration, it represents, in essence, the preaching of the Kingdom on the lines of a theology of salvation—in fact, he echoes the famous 'Jesus proclaimed the Kingdom, and what has come is the Church!' Yes, what has come is the Church, and life in Christ. . . . But if the apostle fought on with never a breathing-space, if he travelled over land and sea, was not that because he was certain that in that Church, however humble and apparently feeble, there lay, for men and nations, not the cruel disappointment of baffled expectation, but the most certain hope? Had he not the assurance that, if the Kingdom had come in the person of Jesus as he walked the roads of Palestine, God was offering to the world, in these churches at Philippi and Corinth where the Spirit had come down, the guarantee of a promise kept?

Paul's thought does not tend to be either speculative or systematic; it was shaped in the Old Testament school, from which he retained an 'object-lesson', learning to celebrate with his people the Lord's great deeds, those of past times as well as those of tomorrow, in order then to look for their theological bearing. So, too, when, on his journeys, he saw the birth of these churches as fruits of the Word and their life 'in the Lord', he tried to discern their meaning, and, looking further and further ahead as he went forward, to understand better, in the community of the brethren, 'the breadth and length and height and depth' of the love of Christ that was already involved in the existence of the smallest church. So one day he came to write, or to suggest to a disciple who handed them on later, the words that we alluded to above: 'For he has made known to us in all wisdom and insight the mystery of his will, according to his purpose which he set forth in Christ as a plan for the fulness of time, to unite all things in him, things in heaven and things on earth' (Eph. 1.9, 10).

The initial impulse for this universal gathering together was given at the time of the cross, where, in the sacrifice of his dying body, Christ effected the reunion of those whose separation had been radical and sacral—Israel and the nations. We cannot now, after twenty centuries of Christianity, surmise what a disrupting revolution in the divine economy this seemed to the first believers, a revolution that was largely unacceptable, as it violated God's holiness by, as they thought, profaning it permanently. Was not the gospel that Paul preached, and found it so hard to get many people to accept, just this, that the cross opened the way to the Father for everyone, without violating his justice? In setting up before us the vision of the new Man in whom the sons of Israel and the children of Hellas are united, as he had been able to see them side by side round the Lord's table in Thessalonica and Ephesus, Paul is conscious of having reached the ultimate secret of the mystery of history; he reads in it the fulfilment of the Word that justified the toil and sufferings of his apostolate. 'The dividing wall of hostility' is broken down; the gate that was jealously guarded by the cherubim is open; here is the reconciliation of the world, a situation so new that its consequences will reverberate throughout the *cosmos*, in things visible and invisible. What schism, what iron curtain, what power could be set against the unity now established, and what man could feel himself to be outside it?

. . . As he had been able to see them united round the Lord's table. If we would find the place where life in Christ was revealed to the apostle, that is where we must come and come again! One evening at Corinth the community is gathered to celebrate the Lord. They have come into the room where they are to meet; the light of smoky lamps shows their faces—slaves, dockers, Crispus the ruler of the synagogue, Gaius, a few women. 'The cup of blessing which we bless, is it not a participation in the blood of Christ? The bread which we break, is it not a participation in the body of Christ? Because there is one loaf, we who are many are one body. . . .' For those whom 'the message of reconciliation' has gathered together this evening, it is at the Lord's table that it is achieved; in his grace Christ makes them his own, together, uniting them in his own Body. Beyond its dreadful chaos, it is here that history converges; here the centuries-old division of Israel and the nations, marked by the wars, curses, and promises that fill the Old Testament, meets the adventure of Graeco-Roman civilization, as those present meet face to face. It is here

Life in Christ and a New Creation

that time with its twofold aspect—irrevocable past and formidable future—is brought back to obedience under one ruler, mastered in the *maranatha*, to be on the one hand forgiven in grace, on the other hand filled with expectation and joy. It is here that space is mastered; here is the heart of the city; they come from the north and the south, from lofty or lowly streets, from the east and the west. . . .

The bread is broken; it is the act of one who came to seek and to save that which was lost; the unpardonable offences, the sufferings, the deadly ills—are they not all gathered together in him and broken with him to become here forgiveness and deliverance and resurrection? As we look at each one, is it not given to us to discover anew the authentic likeness of the Father? As he eats the bread in communion with his Lord, and, in him, with his rediscovered brother, is not each one given his own unity? The many partitions that separated them break down; man is himself re-formed, made whole under the only master, with his body and soul, his mind and heart, his business worries and his fantasies, his wife, his neighbour, and perhaps his enemy; he learns to 'regard no one from a human point of view'; his mind is renewed, as it is trained here to discern the body of Christ and to be open to receive the quite different wisdom of God, who did not choose many of the wise according to worldly standards, or of those who were powerful or of noble birth (I Cor. 2.26); it is initiated into the 'spiritual' reading of events, persons, and things; but his heart, sexuality, will, possessions, and culture are likewise held 'in the Lord', to whom nothing remains foreign.

The Lord is at hand; it is here, indeed, that the Church knows the joy with which the epistles thrill, a joy whose hope lifts up all nature. If everything leads up to this moment, everything in the future proceeds from it, in response to creation's expectation and sighs. At this table the Church is strengthened to carry out its mission, and built up for its service. Some are given as apostles, others as prophets, others as evangelists, and yet others for the service of the saints. The Body becomes alive, the members find out their different tasks, and when they separate they will each one go out as bearers of what they have heard, to bless because they have been blessed, to forgive because they have been forgiven, to offer themselves because they have themselves shared in the consummated sacrifice, and to love with the love with which they first were loved. And how shall we forget the action of Jesus himself on the night that he was betrayed, and the apostle's first thought at the very beginning of each of his letters—that of giving thanks? Is not this the Eucharist, the time when all that God has given to the world in his Son comes back to him in a movement of offering and adoration? 'For this reason I bow my knees before the Father. . . .'

So we are bidden to stay here for a moment longer, as at the beginning of all things as well as the place where they are completed. Life in Christ is not the outcome of nature or theology, but in some way its beginning. No knowledge, either of the world or of history or of the *cosmos*, will bring us by analogy to knowledge of the Body of Christ; on the contrary, participation in the Body will set us on the way to the heart of things.[49] We shall always leave the Lord's table to come back to it; everything comes from it, and everything goes to it.

'Baptism is far from being a kind of sign or symbol, as if there were deeper realities to which it could be related. On the contrary, it is our earthly journeys, or vicissitudes, our changes of place, our terrestrial birth and death themselves, which become quasi-unreal, or rather whose only reality is now derived by reference to the fundamental reality that the sacrament has brought to the heart of things—the new birth. In the same way, since the coming of Christ all food takes on a derived reality by reference to the sacrament, in which it is given as the living bread to the members of the Body.'[50]

Lastly, is not this the source of the difficulties that we experience in giving an account of life in Christ? The analogies by which we rather clumsily try to express it prove, one after the other, to be imperfect, since it is from there that all light comes. We shall probably never be able to say exactly how the body of the risen

---

[49] As we face the major problem of the Church and its mission today—unity—this should teach us that the Lord's Supper ought not by any means to be regarded as the outcome of the efforts towards reunion of those who have received baptism 'into one body', but that it is the cure that is needed for healing the divisions. How are we to know one another, how are we to be trained together to discern the truth, how are we to live in *agapē*, how are we to become one, without the help of 'the same bread'?

[50] This theme is carried to its logical conclusions in a noteworthy article by L. Dallière, 'L'Eglise comme fondement de la réalité humaine', *Le Semeur*, February 1931.

Life in Christ and a New Creation

Lord, while remaining Jesus' body through the breaking of bread, can be identified with the gathered community without confusion or separation, and without tampering with our personalities or degrading his own. Instead of using our poor experience of communication with others, and our notions of identity, we must proceed from the eucharistic and baptismal reality, as the Spirit allows the Church continually to live it anew.

But we must not confine ourselves to a partial reading of I Corinthians 10! The events of the Exodus 'were written down for our instruction, upon whom the end of the ages has come. Therefore let any one who thinks that he stands take heed lest he fall . . .' (11, 12). Having called to mind the infinite riches of grace that he has given us, we must remember that the Church will never be anything but God's people on the march towards the coming of the Lord. What is served on the table does not belong to the Church, which has received it so that it may share it. From the day when it tries to monopolize it so as to keep it to itself it corrupts and loses it, like the manna in the desert. More than one thorn in the flesh will be needed for the Church not to be 'too elated by the abundance of revelations', more than one trial for it not to mistake the earthen vessel for the treasure that it contains—'What we preach is not ourselves, but Jesus Christ as Lord', even though 'the life of Jesus may be manifested in our mortal flesh'.

Nunquam triumphans, semper militans: that is the calling and the glory of the Church in Jesus Christ, in the service and in the company of men, to the end, to the praise of him who has called it to the communion of his well-beloved Son, and whose faithfulness is its only guarantee.

CONCLUSION

We stop here, too early, or perhaps too late; what bounds could be set to an examination that ultimately takes in the whole of Paul's writings? Every line could have been analysed for its bearing on our subject, and sometimes the most unpretentious texts turn out to be the most fruitful. We have constantly had the feeling of being in that privileged place where a man's life and thought meet. And yet one would say that *in Christo* is not made the object of special teaching or special attention; Paul never thought of dealing with it in his letters as a separate subject, so much is it involved in his whole being. Rather than forming one particular item in his theological inventory, it is the light that illuminates the others, the inward movement that quickens them, the gushing spring that makes them fertile. So whatever place we give to the expression, it is not a panacea that allows us to solve all the problems with which Paul's letters still confront us today. We may have been able to analyse the different elements of *in Christo* which, when blended together, make up the whole; but in every passage where we meet the expression, its shade of meaning is so affected by the context as to enrich the latter. Strictly speaking, from an abstract point of view, it means nothing in itself; it always needs the appeal of particular circumstances to take shape and receive its extraordinary fulness.

In being taken to the heart of Paulinism, we are thereby taken to the cross-roads of Judaism and the Graeco-Roman world. Set as a witness of the gospel at that meeting-point, Paul was able to bring both sides their answer in the same words, his own answer. Not that he gave way to the temptation to synthesize so as to give both sides an illusory satisfaction. But he succeeded in going right to the heart of the mystery of Jesus, and in grasping the ultimate range of the cross and the resurrection, which contained the treasures of wisdom. Beyond all systems and accommodations, he succeeded in making plain the bond between the events that had just taken place and the outpouring of the Spirit. In Christ we share in him who is the same yesterday, today, and for ever. Jesus'

Conclusion

death and resurrection fulfilled the promise of the old covenant as well as the mysterious expectation of the Gentiles, and answered the sighs of creation; henceforth everything is embodied in him; in him there meet the various threads of revelation; God's plan is summed up and at the same time goes on anew. In him there culminate the kingly, priestly, and prophetic successions; in him there meet and unite, without impairment, God and man, Israel and Church, law and gospel, judgment and grace, institution and event, creation and redemption, tradition and inspiration, continuity and newness, worship and history, truth and life, ethics and mystical communion, the spiritual and the material, the visible and the invisible, the daily and the eternal, the most interdependent and the most independent existence, all personal responsibility, universal dimensions and intimate relationship.

Paul's greatness consists in having been able to remain at that summit from which the mountain sides fall away, in having held to the top of the ridge. Unfortunately his successors have too often gone down the slopes on one side or the other, and afterwards occupied themselves with only one aspect of revelation, the others remaining unseen in the shadow. We can join Paul, and be found true to his gospel, only by rediscovering the fulness of life in Christ. What the apostle revealed to us of that life can never be sufficiently contemplated and pondered over in our day. It is now, in fact, that the Church of the twentieth century, on the march towards the Kingdom, finds itself once again at the main crossroads. It seems to be going through a salutary change of environment, and now, above all, it needs to know 'that which is in Christ'. In him lies the path of ecumenism towards a regained unity. In him, too, the Church will receive the way of life and the word of testimony that will enable it to fulfil its mission to this fascinating and disordered world in which it is the ambassador of reconciliation. In him it is made ready to face the acceleration of time and the cosmic widening of human history: who, today, cannot see the nations' routes converging? And who knows where they will meet? In Christ . . . but even these words are nothing but a noisy gong or a clanging cymbal if we have not love. That is where everything begins.

BIBLIOGRAPHY
of the principal works consulted

J. Baruzi, *Création religieuse et pensée contemplative*, Paris, 1951; Part I: *La mystique paulinienne et les données autobiographiques des épîtres*

W. Bousset, *Kyrios Christos* (Forschungen zur Religion und Literatur des A und NT 21), 2nd ed., Göttingen, 1921

H. Böhlig, 'In Kyrio', in *Neutestamentliche Studien G. Heinrici dargebracht* (Untersuchungen zum NT 6), Leipzig, 1914

C. Bricka, *Le fondement christologique de la morale paulinienne* (Cahiers de la RHPR 6), Strasbourg, 1923

F. Büchsel, ' "In Christus" bei Paulus', *ZNW* 42, 1949, pp. 141–58

R. Bultmann, *Theology of the New Testament*, ET, 2 vols, 1952–5

L. Cerfaux, *The Church in the Theology of St Paul*, ET, 1959

O. Cullmann, *Christ and Time*, ET, rev. ed., 1962
  The Christology of the New Testament, ET, rev. ed., 1963

W. D. Davies, *Paul and Rabbinic Judaism*, London, 1948

A. Deissmann, *Die neutestamentliche Formel 'in Christo Jesu'*, Marburg, 1892
  Paul: a Study in Social and Religious History, ET, 1912

J. Dupont, *ΣΥΝ ΧΡΙΣΤΩΙ. L'union avec le Christ suivant saint Paul*; Vol. I: '*Avec le Christ*' *dans la vie future*, Bruges, 1952

M. Ferrier-Welti, *La transmission de l'Evangile:* recherche sur la relation personnelle dans l'Eglise d'aprés les épîtres pastorales (ETR), Montpellier, 1957

M. Goguel, *Trois études sur la pensée religieuse du christianisme primitif* (Cahiers de la RHPR 23), Paris, 1931
  La foi à la résurrection de Jésus dans le christianisme primitif, Paris, 1933

J. Héring, *Le Royaume de Dieu et sa venue*, Paris, 1937

E. Lohmeyer, *Kyrios Christos: Eine Untersuchung zu Phil.* 2.5–11 (Sitzungsbericht der Heidelberger Akademie . . . 1927–8, 4. Abhandlung), Heidelberg, 1928
  Grundlagen paulinischer Theologie (Beiträge zur historischen Theologie 1), Tübingen, 1929

E. Mersch, *Le corps mystique du Christ, études de théologie historique*, 2nd ed., Paris, 1936

F. Neugebauer, 'Das paulinische "In Christo" ', *NTS* 4, 1957–8, pp. 124–38

Bibliography

E. Percy, *Der Leib Christi*, Lund, 1942
T. Preiss, *La vie en Christ*, Neuchâtel, 1951; partial ET, *Life in Christ* (Studies in Biblical Theology 13), 1957
H. Schlier, *Christus und die Kirche im Epheserbrief*, Tübingen, 1930
W. Smauch, *In Christus. Eine Untersuchung zur Sprache und Theologie des Paulus* (NT Forschungen I 9), Gütersloh, 1935
O. Schmitz, *Die Christusgemeinschaft des Paulus im Lichte seines Genitivgebrauches* (NT Forschungen I 2), Güterlsoh, 1924
A. Schweitzer, *The Mysticism of Paul the Apostle*, ET, 1931
E. Schweizer, *Erniedrigung und Erhöhung bei Jesus und seinen Nachfolgern* (Abhandlung zur Theologie des A und NT 28), Zürich, 1955; partial ET, *Lordship and Discipleship* (Studies in Biblical Theology 28), 1960
H. von Soden, *Sakrament und Ethik bei Paulus* (Marburger theologische Studien 1), Gotha, 1931
L. S. Thornton, *The Common Life in the Body of Christ*, 2nd ed., 1944
A. Wikenhauser, *Die Christusmystik des heiligen Paulus* (Biblische Zeitfragen XII, 8–10), 2nd ed., 1956

INDEX OF AUTHORS

Afanassieff, N., 104
Allmen, J. J. von, 61, 112

Barth, K., 28, 64
Baruzi, J., 21, 23, 41, 46, 62
Behm, J., 29
Benoit, P., 96, 102, 103, 105
Blass, F., 93
Bonhoeffer, D., 60, 90
Bonnard, P., 20, 55, 57, 64, 65, 68, 72, 73, 79, 85, 89, 99
Bricka, C., 53
Brunner, E., 70
Bultmann, R., 16, 29, 71, 78, 84, 102
Butte, A., 79, 97, 98

Calvin, J., 39, 61, 70
Carrez, M., 81, 82
Cerfaux, L., 24, 105
Chevallier, M. A., 51
Cullmann, O., 20, 22, 70, 82, 85, 89, 96, 101, 103, 104, 108

Dallière, L., 116
Deissmann, A., 53
Deissner, K., 27
Delling, G., 76, 81, 82
Dibelius, M., 68, 88, 96
Dupont, J., 26, 35, 36, 38, 78

Ferrier-Welti, M., 56
Foerster, W., 97

Goguel, M., 20

Hatzfeld, H., 90
Hauck, F., 66, 76
Haupt, E., 81

Héring, J., 22, 36, 39, 56, 70, 72, 73, 93, 94, 95, 97, 99, 108, 109

Käsemann, E., 102
Kierkegaard, S., 48
Kittel, G., 23, 74
Kümmel, W. G., 53, 56, 69, 79, 96

Lagrange, M. J., 57
Leenhardt, F. J., 19, 34, 87, 98
Lietzmann, H., 22, 79, 85, 96, 110
Lohmeyer, E., 26, 76, 79
Loisy, A., 15
Luther, M., 18, 19, 39, 77, 111

Masson, C., 23, 53, 81, 87, 88, 95, 96, 97, 102
Menoud, P. H., 24, 94, 95
Mersch, E., 47
Michaelis, W., 53, 57, 58, 76, 82
Munck, J., 83, 84

Nygren, A., 89

Oepke, A., 76, 82, 93

Pascal, B., 106
Percy, E., 59, 81, 102, 109
Philibert, M., 27
Preiss, Th., 18, 34, 46, 61, 74, 103
Prunet, O., 89

Reitzenstein, R., 27
Rendtorff, R., 81
Rietschel, E., 69
Robinson, J. M., 21, 56

Schlatter, A., 81
Schlier, H., 76, 102

Index of Authors

Schmidt, K. L., 105
Schneider, J., 74
Schweitzer, A., 15, 21, 22, 35, 58, 61, 68, 74, 77, 85, 113
Schweizer, E., 30, 69
Soden, H. von, 60, 70, 97
Soucek, J. B., 94

Spicq, C., 84
Stauffer, E., 85, 86, 89

Thornton, L. S., 62

Windisch, H., 23, 72, 78, 79, 80, 96

INDEX OF BIBLICAL REFERENCES

OLD TESTAMENT

Exodus
4.22   98

Numbers
3.12   98
4.1, 2   98

Numbers
8.18   98

Deuteronomy
18.13   27

I Kings
11.4   27

Isaiah
42   89

Ezekiel 66

NEW TESTAMENT

Matthew
7.14   77
12.18   89
16   56
24.22   76, 82

Mark
5.26   74

Luke
5.31, 32 85
13.2   75
13.29   99

John
5–7   57
13.34   96
14–17   57
15.12   89

Acts
6.7   28
9.16   75, 82
9.18–19   77
11.24   59
14.22   82

Romans
1.3–4   21
1.7   89

Romans
1.8   51
1.17   23
1.21   51
3.6   51
3.21   50
4.17   50
5   33
5.3   77
5.5   88
5.8   33, 50, 85
5.10   85
6   33, 39, 60, 94
6.3ff.   24, 34, 35
6.5   34, 35
6.10   100
6.11, 23 51
7.5   75
7.6   95
8   24, 43, 46, 52, 87, 98
8.9, 11   42
8.14   51
8.17, 23 98
8.28   23
8.28–30   25
8.29   19, 23, 52, 98
8.31–39   87
8.32   85, 87
8.35   76

Romans
8.39   51
9–11   65
9.3   79
9.11   68
9.20   50
12.1   51, 65
12.2   27, 65
12.3, 4, 6ff. 65
12.13   60
12.16   65
13.8–10   88
13.11   28
14   66, 110
14.4   66
14.7, 8   66, 71
14.8   100
14.10–12 51
14.11   51
14.14   60
14.23   111
15.5   53, 65
15.6   51
15.7   69, 89
15.10, 19 83
15.16   97
15.30   87
16.5   97
16.17   27

Index of Biblical References

I Corinthians
1–4	50
1.9	51
1.13	78
1.18	72
1.21	51
2	27
2.5	27
2.6	24
2.11f.	52
2.12	51
2.26	115
3.1	24
3.1–2	27
3.10	51
3.16	42
3.16–20	108
3.21	62
3.22, 23	100
4.6	56
4.8	37
4.8–13	19, 56
4.9	19
4.13	79
4.15b–17	56
4.16	53
5.6–8	96
5.12–13	27
6	42
6.2–3	27
6.7	109
6.9, 10	97
6.12ff.	109
6.15, 19	42
6.20	51
7	112
8	110
8.1	88
8.2	37
8.3	87
8.6	50
9.20f.	57
9.21	10, 66
9.26f.	37
10	60, 117
10–11	69
10.11, 12	117

I Corinthians
10.15	27
11	70
11.1	53, 56
11.3	100
11.12	50
11.13, 28–31	27
12.12	59, 80
12.13	5, 66, 67
12.26	80
13	19, 85, 88
13.10, 11	27
13.13	86
14.20	27
14.26	86
15	99, 105
15.1–9	43
15.3–5	21
15.16	98
15.19f.	38
15.20–23	97
15.28	51, 99
15.31	62, 78
16.14	88
16.15	97

II Corinthians
1.3	51
1.4	80
1.5ff.	74, 80
1.7	60, 79
1.14	62
1.22	97
2.14	19
3	19
3.1	93
3.9	23
3.14	95
3.17	44
3.18	23, 26
4.2	93
4.5	44
4.10	22, 78
4.11	22, 72, 78
4.12	72, 78
4.16	22

II Corinthians
4.16, 17	21
4.16ff.	78
4.17	23
5	26
5.5	97
5.6	37
5.12	93
5.14	49, 88, 93
5.16	44, 47, 94, 95
5.17	5, 17, 92, 93, 94
5.18	50
6.3–10	19
6.4	93
7.3	71
7.11	93
8.6	60
8.24	62
9.10	50
10–13	73
10.15	27
10.12–18	93
11.2	49
11.17	53
12	21, 41
12.11	93
13.5	27, 43
13.11	65

Galatians
1	16
1.1	50
1.12, 15	43
2.20	43, 46, 85
3.2	47
3.16	97
3.26–29	5, 66, 67, 97
4.4	50
4.4–5	21
4.5f.	51
4.12	53, 57
4.12, 19	48
4.14	50
4.19	25, 43, 84
5.6	88, 92
5.13, 14	88

Index of Biblical References

Galatians	
5.15	64
5.21	97
5.22	87
5.24	75
6.4	27
6.10	88, 89
6.14	62
6.15	92, 93

Ephesians	
1–2	40
1.9, 10	113
1.15	88
1.17	87
1.23	99
2.6	39
2.11ff.	83
2.15	29
2.21	28, 100
3	87
3.6	97
3.13	84
3.14–21	87
3.17	42, 43, 49
3.18	87
4.8	40
4.11	51
4.13	24, 28
4.15	28
4.16	61, 88, 100
4.23	27
4.24	28, 29
5	102
5.1	53, 57
5.2	85
5.5	97
5.10, 15, 17	27
5.22ff.	49

Philippians	
1.4	60
1.5	28, 100
1.8	49
1.9	27, 29
1.12–14	79
1.18–20	29

Philippians	
1.21	34
1.23	36
1.25	27, 63
1.26	62
1.29	75
2	17f., 21, 57, 63, 64
2.1	64
2.2	63, 64
2.3	64
2.5	17, 34, 64
2.5–11	21
2.7	34
2.9	50, 64
2.13	50
2.16	62
2.17	79
2.17–19, 27	63
3	16–18, 21, 67
3.3ff.	62
3.4–21	5
3.8f.	37
3.10, 11, 12–15, 21	17
3.12, 15	27
3.17	53
3.17, 18	55
3.20	29
3.21	18, 36
4.2	64
4.4f.	63
4.9	53, 55
4.20	51

Colossians	
1.4	88
1.6	26, 100
1.12	97
1.15	23, 98
1.18	98
1.22, 24, 25	82, 83
1.24	5, 74, 76, 79, 81, 82
1.27	43, 83

Colossians	
1.28	24, 27, 83
2.3	40
2.16, 17	95
2.19	28, 100
3	40, 41
3.1–4	40
3.3	39
3.9–11	5, 66
3.9–12	28
3.10	68
3.11	29, 68, 99
3.12	89
3.13	69
3.14	28, 88
4.5	27

I Thessalonians	
1.3	86
1.6	52, 53, 54
2.8	71, 89
2.14	51–54, 75
2.19f.	63
3.5	86
3.8	71
3.11	51
3.12	27, 88
4.9	88
4.16	51

II Thessalonians	
1.3	27
1.7	77
2.6, 7	82
2.13	89
2.16	85
3.7–9	53, 55

Philemon	
5	88
6	29
16	89

I Peter	
1.8	39
5.5	111

I John	
4.10	85

www.ingramcontent.com/pod-product-compliance
Lightning Source LLC
Chambersburg PA
CBHW050838160426
43192CB00011B/2076